Fallen
 Star

A Return to Self through the Eight Limbs of Yoga

Fallen ✳ Star

Molly Chanson

Nine Rivers
Brunswick, Maine

Fallen Star

A Return to Self through the Eight Limbs of Yoga

Published by Nine Rivers,
an imprint of Shanti Arts Publishing

Cover and interior design by Shanti Arts Designs

Cover and interior artwork by Anne Chanson

Shanti Arts LLC
Brunswick, Maine
www.shantiarts.com

Printed in the United States of America

This book is a memoir, written from the author's recollections
of experiences that occurred over several years. The dialogue
presented in this book is not intended to represent word-
for-word transcripts; events and scenes are not precise
representations. The names and characteristics of some
individuals have been changed to protect privacy. In
all cases, the author has remained true to the feeling
and meaning of what happened and what was said.

ISBN: 978-1-956056-29-7 (softcover)
ISBN: 978-1-956056-30-3 (digital)

Library of Congress Control Number: 2022934939

for my Mom,
my first yoga teacher

Contents

The Eight Limbs of Yoga

The Yamas

Ahimsa : Nonviolence

Satya : Truth

Asteya : Nonstealing

Bramacharya : Nonexcess

Aparigraha : Nongrasping

The Niyamas

Saucha : Purity

Santosha : Contentment

Tapas : Self-discipline

Svadhyaya : Self-study

Ishvara pranidhana : Surrender

Pranayama : Breath

Pratyahara : Presence

Dharana : Focus

Dhyana : Meditation

Samadhi : Enlightenment

Sanskrit Words Defined

Asana : Pose

Agnistambhasana : Fire Log

Anahatasana : Heart Opener

Ardha Chandrasana : Half Moon

Baddha Konasana : Bound Angle

Baddha Virabhadrasana : Humble Warrior

Bakasana : Crow

Balasana : Child

Catur Svanasana : Dolphin

Dandasana : Staff

Garudasana : Eagle

Kapotasana : Pigeon

Malasana : Garland

Matsyasana : Fish

Parivritta Trikonasana : Revolved Triangle

Parshva Virabadhrasana : Side Warrior

Patita Tarasana : Fallen Star

Phalakasana : Plank Pose

Pincha Mayurasana : Forearm Stand

Sansangasana : Rabbit

Sarvangasana : Shoulder Stand

Savasana : Corpse

Trikonasana : Triangle

Utkatasana : Chair
Utkata Konasana : Goddess
Uttana Shishosana : Puppy
Virabadhrasana : Warrior

Pranayama : Breath Control
Kapalabhati : Skull-shining
Dirgha : Three-part

Ahara : Vehicle of Consciousness
Dharma : Nature of Reality; Soul's Purpose
Dhristi : Focused Gaze
Granthi : Knot; Doubt
Mudra : Ritual Gesture
Nadis : Channels
Sadhana : Daily Practice
Samskara : Mental Impressions; Imprints

Foreword

by Stephen Cope

F OR ALMOST THREE THOUSAND YEARS, THE YOGA TRADITIONS IN INDIA
have been mightily obsessed with two thorny questions: What is the
nature of human suffering? What is an optimal human life?

First, of course, comes the question of suffering. Precisely why and
how does a human being suffer? Can suffering be attenuated or even
eliminated? If so, how? If not, why not? Are there some forms of suffering
that we all must simply endure?

Sigmund Freud was interested in this very same problem. After gradually
developing his own brilliant technique for psychological healing, which he
called psychoanalysis, he explained that his technique "is to help the patient
relinquish neurotic suffering and return to a state of ordinary unhappiness."
Ordinary unhappiness? Really? Can't get rid of that, too, Dr. Freud?

Yogis, as it turned out, were interested precisely in what Freud called
"ordinary unhappiness." And they believed that they had, indeed, found a
remedy for it.

So, having worked through the issues of suffering, these intrepid yogis
went on to examine the question of optimal living. What does it look like
when a human being is functioning at absolutely full capacity? What are
the peak physical, spiritual, and psychological possibilities inherent in
our human makeup? And are these extraordinary human potentials open
to anyone willing to make the requisite effort?

Across the ages, the yogis' search for answers has been wildly productive.
It has led the ancient yogis to cobble together a reliable path to full human
life—what is sometimes in the yoga tradition called *jivan mukti* or "the soul
awake in this lifetime." The path is detailed. It is practical. It is systematic.
And it is open to anyone with the motivation to walk it to the end. It is also,
apparently, timeless, for it has really not changed significantly for millenia.

The ancients called this path the Noble Way or the Royal Road
because it was known to reliably lead ordinary individuals to become
truly noble specimens of humanity.

After many centuries of experimentation and development, this path
was finally systematized and written down by a great sage probably named
Patanjali, who lived and taught and wrote in India in the first or second
century of what we now call the Common Era. This remarkable sage most

likely directed an academy that instructed generations of aspirants in the time-tested methods of yoga. He wrote the first full scale exegesis of the path and called it the *Yoga Sutras*, meaning the Threads of Yoga.

Now, this Patanjali was a seriously smart dude and was probably fully enlightened to boot. Nonetheless, in putting together his book, he could have profited from some editorial help. It is virtually impossible to really follow his teachings without a guide, without a commentary, without help. So in every age and time since he penned the *Yoga Sutras*, teachers and commentators have risen up to help struggling human beings make sense of this path and to implement it in their oh-so-very-human struggles.

By and large, these teachers, these commentators have been "of their time." They have themselves been immersed in the particular suffering of the age in which they lived. They have walked the path themselves. They have struggled. And, to some extent, they have "awakened."

Now comes Ms. Molly Chanson. She is a contemporary yogini who has struggled, studied, practiced, become frustrated, left practice, returned to practice, sought out teachers, and read extensively the ancient documents of yoga. And like other commentators through the ages, she brings us the fruit of her own particular struggle with the path. And the fruit of all her work turns out to be exactly what we need. Her commentary on the Royal Road of Yoga is colorful, engaging, detailed, real, accessible, and very much "of our time." It is written in contemporary language. Indeed, it often reads like a novel, which is a delight. Her novelistic style keeps us reading. It keeps us wondering: how will it all come out? How will this story end?

Many contemporary yogis will be very glad to have Molly's new book, *Fallen Star*, and thereby to take her on as a reliable guide—time-tested. Above all, in my opinion, her work gives us what we most need: encouragement—encouragement to persist on the path. She successfully makes us believe that if she can do it, we can too.

So, dear reader, dive in!! And profit.

Stephen Cope
Senior Scholar Emeritus
Kripalu Center
Stockbridge, Massachusetts
Spring 2021

Introduction

A S HUMANS WE HAVE A DESIRE TO BE WHOLE, TO LIVE OUR BEST LIFE, and to fulfill our purpose. This leads us to desire certain people, circumstances, life stages, or body types. But external desires cannot complete us. In yoga, we learn how to be fulfilled internally so we don't rely on external factors to define our self-worth. What someone else does to us is not who we are. What our life looks like on the outside is not who we are. Yoga teaches that we are already whole and already accepted simply because we exist.

Getting to this awareness and actually believing it is a challenge. As a woman, I constantly rely on other people and outside appearance to sustain me, to validate my existence. I seek approval from others to determine my worth.

In my twenties, I attended an intense Ashtanga yoga class religiously. I moved my body through the set sequence, the same series of poses, for an hour and a half. The class was held in a gym, and I listened to runners stomp around the rubber track above as I sweated and pushed my body through the strenuous sequence. Something about getting through the intense poses each time transformed my mind and the way I saw myself. By the time we laid down in savasana, my aching muscles and wet body melted into the mat. I craved my Ashtanga class, not only for the physical changes I saw taking place in my body but for the intense presence I felt while breathing through each pose. I appreciated the meditative experience of letting my outside world go and coming to sit on my mat. I felt held and free at the same time.

Of course, a strong body will come. When you regularly participate in a yoga practice, you can be assured that a healthier, stronger, more attractive body will emerge from that discipline. But the physical appearance does not define you. And that's true with anything external that you might look to in order to define who you are—marriage, motherhood, a perfect yoga body. When you let go of the outcome, there are no successes or failures, there is only the journey.

I wrote this book while going though my divorce as well as recovery from alcohol addiction. Needless to say, in addition to writing as a way to heal, I was reading numerous spiritual and self-help books. I read Pema Chödrön's book *When Things Fall Apart,* and a line immediately jumped out at me. I wrote it down in my notebook. I wrote it on a Post-it and stuck it to my bedroom wall. I will never forget her words: "The path is the goal."

When you first set out on a path, you probably can't see the end of the dark tunnel. You may feel lost and unsure. I can't say what the end will look like for you, but I can say, based on my own experience, that the end result doesn't matter. You can't make a wrong turn. The only way to screw up is to not be present along the path. To heal and to feel complete, the path is the goal.

MY START

I stepped into the familiar brick building on Broad Street for the first time in over six months. The vegetarian cafe and juice bar had closed and reopened as a coffee shop and bike showroom; round tables and hippie decor had been replaced with sleek wooden benches and graphic posters on the walls. Nitro-brewed coffee came out of a tap and the new owner's yellow lab wandered comfortably around the back of the store. The stage where local musicians held their open mics now displayed pastries and protein bars behind a curved, glass case.

I ordered a regular hot coffee (no room for cream) and headed upstairs to the redesigned loft. When a steep rent increase forced my friend's cafe to close, the yoga studio also lost its space upstairs. After several months of renovations, the storefront was finally back open for business, and despite my conflicted emotions about the space closing, I longed to re-enter the yoga sanctuary upstairs, to feel the warmth of the worn-out floorboards beneath my feet and to see the shadows that danced in the morning sun as it cascaded unashamedly through dirty glass windows.

Out of habit, I almost removed my shoes at the foot of the stairs, but now, there was no need. I remembered the humble space where I had practiced yoga for the last year. I climbed gently and hesitantly up each step, not sure what I would find when I arrived at the top. The first thing I noticed was a parade of pastel-colored trek bikes, angled prettily against the walls and windows. A small, trendy seating area in the center of the room invited customers to sit down and flip through magazines. I glanced at the center wall; the scroll with Buddha's quotes for success was gone. So were the amber rock lamps and carefully placed pillows. The fixture above and the flooring below had both been replaced. Except for the bright sunshine still streaming in through tall glass windows, the room had been transformed.

I felt a sting of grief as I remembered the entire last year. No one would know this space was once used for yoga. No one would know that the scent of eggs and vegan bacon wafted upstairs, intermingling with our burning sage and lavender oils, as we mindfully moved our bodies through poses. No one would know I came to this room initially to escape, but that it slowly became my sacred ritual and a way to discover myself. Looking back, even though I had tried to run away, the daily yoga practice actually pointed me straight toward the fire I was meant to walk through.

On paper my life looked pretty good. I was married and the mother of two young boys, lived in a nice house, and ran a successful business. But something was off, and it nagged at me persistently.

Have you ever looked around at the toys on the floor, the dishes in the sink, and the tiny handprints on the walls and wondered, *Did I really manifest this? Is this the life I asked for?* We can look around at all the mess and chaos of motherhood and still see the beauty in it. But sometimes, there is also an inner voice telling us that something is wrong. This is the startle that wakes you up in the middle of the night. This is the knot that forms in your stomach when you're at the grocery store picking up chicken for dinner. This is the moment of clarity that creeps into your mind when you're looking at your husband and think, *Does he see me? Does he know me at all?*

So I came back to my lost yoga practice and committed to it every day for a year. I used to do yoga as a form of exercise in my twenties, but since having babies, I had let my practice go, temporarily at first, but then it became permanent. If anything, I was using yoga as a way to run away from my problems. It was time to be with myself, time to forget about all the ugliness going on at home and in my marriage. And isn't that how a self-care routine often starts? Out of desperation? Nothing ever seems like a good enough reason to start putting ourselves first. Often, we start before we are ready. We start before we even understand why. Sometimes, when we can't stand it anymore, we just START.

Some days I had to force myself to go to yoga. And once there, I often felt like leaving early. I sat on my mat at the beginning of class and thought about all the other tasks I had to do that day. I left my phone on vibrate next to my mat in case the school called about one of the boys. I made lists in my mind upon arriving about all the errands I would complete after class. Some days, I wanted to literally run out of the room. My skin burned and my mind raced, but I made myself stay on my mat, quietly and often painfully abiding.

Moving through each pose, I felt my muscles for the first time in a decade. My thighs quivered relentlessly in warrior pose. My arms wavered at first, but eventually found a sturdy balance in chaturanga. My abdomen wrapped tightly around my entire torso in triangle. For the first time, I understood that we have an integrated core, one that serves our entire stomach and back, not just the flattering abdominals that peak out on the surface. The changes started in my physical body. Carrying my boys upstairs to bed at night became easier. Jeans that pinched in my waist fit more comfortably. Over a few months, yoga class became less of an escape and more of a wellness ritual, a way to honor and take care of myself. Then, after even more practice, yoga became a spiritual practice that taught me to love myself, which I hadn't done in a very long time.

Let's be clear, taking care of yourself is a basic survival instinct. As humans, our priority is our own safety, which includes discovering our inner truth. When you ignore that instinct for too long, pieces of your soul start to die. Sometimes, after years of ignoring your inner self and your inner callings, all the broken pieces you thought you had successfully propped up begin to topple apart, no longer able to withstand being put off or ignored. *I'll get to that problem later; there are more important things to focus on right now. It's selfish to put myself first.*

It's a myth that self-care is selfish. Actually, self-care focused on the soul is self-sacrifice. Because after a regular routine of self-care, there is actually less self than before. A regular self-care ritual will assist in exposing and peeling away layers of the self that aren't serving you in order to get to the true, indestructible parts that exist underneath.

The discoveries I made through yoga are plentiful and profound. I learned to stay even when I wanted to run. I learned to accept and forgive my addiction. I learned that my marriage ending wasn't the worst thing in the world. I learned that I was strong enough to float in warrior three pose and also strong enough to make it through my divorce. I was strong. I was enough.

How did I know to intuitively start a yoga practice when I was confused? When I was lost in my marriage and in my roles as a woman? What is yoga? How do the physical poses leak into our lives and our minds even when we don't pay attention? I've spoken with many women who have done the same; they sought out yoga when they didn't know what else to do. When we break open during difficult times, the parts we let fall away heal us. As we put ourselves back together, we gain depth, vulnerability, strength, resilience, self-compassion, forgiveness, and most of all, LOVE. We are never the same as we once were; we are like an ancient tree that has grown gracefully into deep roots and thick branches, nicked and gnarled, but more majestic and eye-catching than the sapling.

Without my practice, I would have crumbled apart, but I wouldn't have come back together. Like my abdominal muscles that are now wrapped tightly around my core, I no longer sacrifice truth for the imaginary; I no longer bury depth and knowledge under a glittery facade. I unraveled the surface, and I found my indestructible self.

PATANJALI'S EIGHT LIMBS OF YOGA

The Eight Limbs of Yoga are a set of principles that, when put into practice, create a fulfilled and complete life. The limbs are not a religion, although, if you do believe in a particular doctrine, you will find many similarities. Throughout this book, I use the Eight Limbs of Yoga as a template for my life story, and I invite you to explore them as a means to a more complete way of life for yourself—a life of presence, compassion, resilience, and an ability to trust your innate wisdom.

You can visualize the eight limbs as equal branches on the same tree or as symmetrical petals around the same flower. The limbs are not a hierarchy. Rather, they are circular, meaning we can be inside all the limbs at the same time. You do not need to complete one limb in order to move on to the next. In my experience, the limbs are fluid and also dependent on one another.

Throughout this book, I will refer to yoga philosophy as a teacher for our everyday life experience, the meaningful and the mundane. I have seen the principles of the eight limbs as they weave throughout my stories, and their lessons have helped me to make profound meaning of my individual experience. I'm excited to share my journey with you, which started long before I became a wife and mom. My story might take place in a different city than yours, with different people and circumstances, but at our heart, our indestructible center, we are not different. In fact, if not for our individual experiences, we are all the same and therefore not separate at all.

Wherever you are on your life path, and for whatever reason you picked up this book, there is no limit to how far you can go. You are capable of more than you currently know. You are already accepted. You are already whole. And once you know this for yourself, once you experience this deep understanding of self-love, self-acceptance, and overall worthiness, you will feel a freedom and peace like no other. You will be unshakable and able to accept emotions in a way you resisted before. You will act out of compassion for yourself instead of fear. You will be able to listen to your heart and trust what it says. Life won't be perfect, but it's amazing how much better and more manageable life is when you don't rely on someone else to define your experience.

Like yoga, life is a practice, so let's begin with an open heart, an open mind, and the compassion we deserve, as we unravel much of what has been taught to us about life. Let us embark on a new way of living.

BALASANA : CHILD'S POSE

PART I

The Five Yamas

MORAL RESTRAINTS : AM I GOOD?

"When even one virtue becomes our nature,
the mind becomes clean and tranquil. Then
there is no need to practice meditation; we
will automatically be meditating always."

—Sri Swami Satchidananda

ONE

Ahimsa : Nonviolence

"In the chaotic rubble, she still remembered who she was."

—R. M. Drake

I AM ELEVEN, RESTING ON THE SMALL SLOPE OF GROUND BY THE TENNIS courts near our summer cottage. On my back, knees bent, I playfully tap one foot and then the other, and squint at flashes of sunshine that break through passing clouds. A cold lump of hard dirt presses annoyingly into the small of my back, so I shift my body to the left and brush my fingertips along blades of evenly cut grass. I miss summer and my friends. I just started fifth grade at a new school, and I feel more connection to the summer cottage and its surroundings than anything at home.

My family has come up to Lake Geneva just for the day. I am alone. Open space surrounds me; mature pine trees line the edges of the lawn and create a barrier between the protected neighborhood and the busy road on the other side. The creek rushes steadily downhill and toward the lake. This sloped spot on the earth holds and supports me. When I finally close my eyes, twinkles of greenish light flash in the center of my forehead as my sight adjusts from bright daylight to a darkness inside. My parents will say it's time to get back in the car soon. I keep my eyes closed for as long as I can and try to remember who I am.

The first yama is ahimsa, which means "non-violence." This first yama is said to be the foundation and the true practice from which all eight limbs of yoga can be achieved. As humans, if we could master the practice of non-violence, no other yoga or meditation practices would be needed.

To practice ahimsa means we practice non-violence to all living beings, including animals, people, the Earth, and ourselves. Even if we consider ourselves to be nonviolent people, violence plays out in subtle ways both on our yoga mats and in daily life. Critical self-talk, unforgivingness, judgment, eating disorders, and addictions are examples of how we turn violent toward ourselves. We hold onto expectations of what we want our world to be like, and we react uncompassionately when life doesn't go our way. We blame ourselves. We blame others. We grab at the illusion of control, thinking it will bring relief.

BALASANA

I N YOGA WE REST IN BALASANA—CHILD'S POSE. WE BOW OUR BODY TO SIT ON our heels, lower our forehead, and place our arms in front of us, outstretched but surrendering. We invite the rest. We honor our accomplishments as well as our falls. In the practice of rest, we know there is nothing to do in this moment and that nothing matters beyond this pose. Rest creates a gap between what needs to be done and what is happening right now.

I want rest. I want to let go of my quivering thigh muscles in warrior one, relieve my outstretched arms and let them make contact with the mat. I want to fold my body over itself and feel my heart rate slow in my chest. I want to rest my stomach heavily between my open thighs and surrender my breath, my life force.

I also want answers. I want to know if my husband is cheating. So I seek insight inside the darkness that exists behind closed eyes. Folded over, I breathe. I sense the gap between breaths before allowing the air to come fully in. I pause between the strenuous poses and stretches of life and evaluate the sensations—the shakiness, the fear, the sore muscles, and my heart's stinging pain.

I want to relinquish control and maybe actually listen this time. I focus on my forehead, solid on the ground in front of me. I slowly rock it back and forth and gently massage my third eye to coax awake my intuition. How long have I kept her quiet?

Yamas, the first limb of yoga, are five moral principles for living an ethical life. Moral character serves as a beginning, a foundation upon which to achieve lasting happiness. Before doing any poses, we are fulfilled through our character.

Rather than relying on our inner self to be happy, we tend to rely on objects, roles, and relationships. Our desire to be happy drives our desire to grow up, get married, succeed in a career, buy a house, have children, and discover our purpose in the world. We believe collecting these roles and "good things" will make us happy. However, if we betray ourself along the way, if we ignore the five yamas, no amount of external "goodness" will bring happiness.

When we practice the five yamas—the five restraints—we learn kindness and compassion, not only in how we view and treat others, but maybe more importantly, how we view and treat ourselves. The five yamas are: **ahimsa**: non-violence; **satya**: truthfulness; **asteya**: nonstealing; **brahmacharya**: nonexcess; and **aparigraha**: ungrasping.

Despite good intentions, we likely dishonor and misinterpret all five yamas regularly. Practicing the five yamas starts us on a path of self-awareness, one on which we pay attention to our bodies, our thoughts, and actions. We might discover that in subtle ways, we harm ourselves and others. We see that we violently steal from the earth. We want too much and are never satisfied.

We look outside for things to complete us, without first looking inside ourselves. We get married and decide to have children. We decide not to have children. We can't have children. We choose our career. We juggle a family and a career. We implement date nights and sex nights and girls-night-out nights. We smile sympathetically at women in restaurants as they wrangle screaming babies. Then we go home and cry after opening the baby shower invitation that arrives in the mail. We try to do it all, fulfilling all our roles—wife, mother, lover, sister, daughter, friend. We do not surrender our desires with an open palm, as the fifth yama suggests. Instead, we grasp, we cling, we hang on tightly, and then, when something we want appears to be slipping away, we squeeze even harder, maybe even manipulate the situation to get our way. We grab. We compare. We fail. We fall. We do not get what we want, and we are confused.

In the process of grabbing at all things good, we lose ourselves, we betray our personal truths, and we fall deeper into the false belief that something else, something "new" will fulfill us. We turn outward instead of inward, where a shift in perception, and possibly an admission, exists.

"Hey, girl, you're so thin!" Our instructor Andrea leans in to give me a hug before class starts. "How are you doing?"

"Great!" I answer. "I gave up gluten"—because I feel I need to provide an explanation.

In class I rest in wide-legged child's pose. My knees open to the edges of my mat, my body folds snugly between my thighs, and I focus on my third eye, the center of my forehead as it comes in contact with the hard, wooden floor. Once folded into child's pose, I realize I have wanted this break my entire life. For as long as I can remember, I have wanted to rest, to lie down, refrain from battling, and receive.

I don't realize I am thin, at least not to the point that anyone would notice except me. But it's not the first time this week someone has mentioned my appearance or my eating habits. My mother, the other night at dinner: "What, are you not eating bread?" My sister, walking behind me on our way up the stairs: "You look good, but like you've lost weight." Obviously, I didn't drop overnight. Any weight lost from my body and my face has been gradual. Yet today, and to others, it appears to have happened all at once.

I don't like the eyes on me. I dislike that anyone has noticed anything about my body or my habits. If they comment on my body, my subtle acts of violence against myself are more difficult to hide.

As we move slowly out of child's pose and onto all fours for cat/cow, I tip my chin further toward my chest and allow my eyes to peek back at my stomach. The extra skin droops and smushes together like wilted petals.

I study the limp, hanging mass around my belly button. Pale stretch marks from two pregnancies drag like raked sand across my flesh. The hole from the belly button ring I got while in Spain glares a visible pink hue. For a moment, I consider getting it pierced again, which might look better than the now sagging scar. But then I remember the fat needle that popped into my belly and how badly it hurt and the several glasses of Rioja I consumed before lying down on a strange man's table. I'm not that young college girl anymore, and the dancing house parties, swirling nights at home drinking wine across the counter from my parents, and confusing rides in the back of police cars have begun to catch up with me.

I inhale fully into cow pose and lift my heart upward. I tilt my tailbone and elevate my eyes to the sky. The exhale arrives, and I follow it down and inward, curling my back up like a cat. I close my eyes and tuck my chin as the end of my breath squeezes out. The spot behind my forehead is dark but provides comfort.

I extend my belly down again into cow pose and let my abdomen fill unflatteringly with air. The bloated sensation in my stomach reminds me that I haven't had sex with my husband in seven months. Before curving my spine up again into cat, I open my eyes to look at Andrea, our beautiful yoga instructor, arched perfectly on her mat at the front of the room. Her pony tail is long and blonde. Her butt and thighs curve sumptuously beneath tight leggings.

I suspect my husband David is having an affair and that I must have done something to deserve being cheated on. Of course David would choose another woman with curvier legs and fuller breasts and a less defensive demeanor.

The safety of my yoga mat keeps me temporarily away from my obsessive search for evidence that he is cheating. While David is away on business trips, I frantically dig through drawers that aren't mine. I open shoeboxes and analyze receipts. My months of hunting have turned up no tangible proof, yet I cannot stop. All of my searching is a tireless attempt to validate my own intuition. I want evidence that my husband does not love me because I don't know how else to trust myself.

"Molly, you don't need to have proof to leave your husband," my friend Sadie said to me on the phone one day as I talked her ear off about all the things that annoyed me about David, all the excuses and reasons I had to believe he was cheating. Her response shocked me and made me stop. What she meant was: You can leave your husband if that is how you feel. Your feelings are valid enough.

I can examine my belly or close my eyes. I can talk to my body gently, or I can berate and abuse it like I have most of my life. The violence imposed on women's bodies, both self- and societally inflicted, causes eating disorders, addiction, and a fragmented sense of self. I obsess over my body in a disowned yet possessive way; I give my appearance too much influence and power while simultaneously regarding my body as an object to rail against. Like my compulsive digging for proof of David's affair, I get high on the thrill of the search, but my heart sinks a little each time I think I may have uncovered the truth. Being called out as thin gives me a rush of validation, and so I continue to compare my body with others and disown its traits in order to control and walk about this earth with a sense of purpose. If I loved the way I looked, there would be nothing to fix. If I were satisfied in my marriage, there would be nothing to uncover.

What would it be like to simply exist in the present? I have always been on the hunt for something else, something perfect that will complete me.

The inhale arrives, and we continue the cat/cow movement to the rhythm of our own breath. The stickiness of the mat holds my palms in place as I arch and curl, open and close, breathe in and out. In yoga, my mat keeps me safely grounded in the present moment, at least for glimpses of time, which grants enough relief and peaks my curiosity. I trust my body in the pose. I inquire if my view of the world is true or if the truth is here, inside my body and focused on my breath.

In cat/cow, if I close my eyes, my own inhale and exhale direct my body when to tuck and when to uncurl. Rather than chide myself for what is wrong with my body, the single focus on breath guides my awareness to the strength in my arms and the important muscles that effort behind my abdomen. In the darkness behind my third eye, love and compassion slowly emerge, and I taste their sweet acceptance for what is. I no longer see myself or anyone else in the room. I no longer compare.

After several rounds of cat/cow, the distraction of society dissipates, and the booming critical voice in my mind softens to a whisper. On my mat, I am able to hear: *What if, Molly? What if you are good just as you are?*

TWO

Satya : Truth

"People who are 'nice' hold truth inside until they reach
a breaking point and then they become dangerously
inappropriate; I know because I used to be such a person."

—Deborah Adele

The second yama is satya, which means "truth." We are truthful with
our thoughts, speech, actions, and behaviors. The problem is that some
of our untruths are so embedded in our subconscious and based on
such deep conditioning that we probably don't even know they exist.
We accept the beliefs about ourself and the world as truth even though
they might not be real. Slowly, we begin to lose our ability to trust our
intuition. When we are dishonest with ourself, even a little, our body
knows, and we move further away from who we really are.

Yoga creates an opening for curiosity to enter. We start to ask questions
about ourself and our beliefs, and this new awareness deepens our
understanding of self. We uncover the untruths to get closer to our
core, our true self. When we acknowledge and accept all parts of
ourself, we no longer agree to certain terms that have been dictated
by others or society. We operate in alignment with our own truth,
which lifts the burden of trying relentlessly to be someone we are not.

KAPALABHATI

WHEN I WAS FIFTEEN, MY MOM INTRODUCED ME TO YOGA. WE
practiced every day in our living room when I got home from
school. My mom had done yoga most of her adult life with a group
of women in someone else's living room. Living rooms, like church
basements, became sacred spaces for the seekers, for the broken, for the
curious.

After spending my teenage years in a small town where I couldn't go to the grocery store without running into several people who knew me, I was ecstatic to move to the larger city of Madison for college. My first night at the dorm I walked down the sidewalk past front porches and keg parties and marveled at the fact that no one would call my name.

I was taking an elective dance class and learned that the professor also taught yoga. So on Thursday nights, when no one else used the theater space, we met for our practice.

The night of the first class I stepped into a shadowed doorway wedged between a well-lit coffee shop and a spirited, thumping bar. I walked to the top of the skinny wooden steps that led to a long hallway. On the left, I saw the wing of the large stage below, dark and unlike the brightly lit dance space at 8:30 a.m. On the right, I saw a small doorway where a colorful curtain hung, now pulled off to one side. A soft, pinkish light emerged from the dark room, and three pairs of shoes were lined up neatly outside the door. I removed my sneakers and set them evenly next to the others.

The room was dim. An orange lamp glowed in one corner, and there were a few plants that hid lockers, props, and dance attire. The floor was warm and soft, and we laid our mats on top of the thin, reddish carpet. My instructor invited our bodies into a seated cross-legged pose, and after she guided the exact position of our feet, our sits bones, our shoulders, and our spine, we began a simple breath meditation. After several minutes in stillness with my eyes closed, I was surprised when I noticed my body moving. At the sound of our instructor's voice, I rolled my shoulders in small circles up, back, and down. I tucked my chin and curved my torso, forward and side to side. My breath guided my movement, and before long, all of us were in pigeon pose.

My right leg bent uncomfortably in front of my right hip, and my left leg extended long behind my body. I lifted my torso upright in order to adjust my hips to an even level before folding over my bent front leg. I reached my hands forward, spread my palms and fingers wide, and pulled my torso out and down across my thigh. On my exhale, I placed my forehead on the mat between my outstretched arms. My left hip was relieved, but my right hip screamed at me.

Pigeon is one of the first poses my mom ever taught me. She used to wedge a blanket from the couch under my unwilling hips until I could lean over my front leg and rest my forehead on the carpet in front of me. This, she said, is the most important part—making contact with your third eye, the spot that knows. Since then, whether I need to stack my hands or use a block, I always rest my forehead on a hard surface and close my eyes to hear the wisdom inside me.

Breathing through a difficult pose to create space in our lungs and minds is where forgiveness, understanding, and truth are allowed to enter. With my forehead on my mat and my right hip yelling, I breathed in hot fear. I exhaled cool understanding out of O-shaped lips. The steady line of air mimicked the breeze that rushed by outside and shook thawing bare tree branches getting ready to push out new buds after the long winter.

The instructor prompted us to move out of pigeon. She told us to engage our palms on the mat and press ourselves into three-legged dog, which is downward-facing dog with one leg raised. Enthusiastically, I lifted my hips off the mat by leaning forward into my hands and wrists. I picked up my knee and pressed my whole body back and up into three-legged dog with my right leg raised. As soon as my left heel hit the mat and my arms straightened all the way back into the pose, I tipped my hips to the right and flopped my right heel toward my tailbone. My hip released and opened. The dull ache from staying in pigeon became a luxurious stretch through my entire right side.

"Breathe into the spaces where you feel tension. Inhale into that spot, and exhale to release." Our instructor allowed us time to shake out our hips and play in the pose. I liked the opportunity to move and sway amid the darkness outside. I liked hearing students with backpacks walking on the sidewalk below and boisterous patrons entering and leaving the bar. I noticed the groan of buses on the street as they pulled over briefly to pick up passengers and then continued on. I liked the secret yoga space we had claimed. The world clamored outside, but I wanted to remain here, on my mat, eyes closed, inside my breath, and stoking the yoga fire inside my core.

The following Thursday I returned to the yoga class. I came down to my mat and my seat and closed my eyes as the other students entered the room. Our instructor explained that tonight we would begin our practice with some rounds of kapalabhati, a pranayama—skull-shining breath. I had no idea what she was talking about. Curious and excited, I pointed the crown of my head taller in my cross-legged position and sat completely alert with a reaching spine.

To practice kapalabhati, you exhale fast through the nostrils while you push your stomach forcefully back toward your spine. You let the inhale remain passive, like a rebound, rather than control the air taken in. The focus is on the exhale and the pumping of the stomach—again and again and again. The technique in English is called skull-shining breath because it cleans the respiratory channels and polishes the mind, like wiping down unused silver to reveal a shiny, reflective surface. During kapalabhati, dust and grime are scrubbed away, and our mind becomes clear.

When we practiced kapalabhati in the small, carpeted space, our collective breath in the room was fast as a heartbeat. Our forceful exhales sounded like billows pumping air onto a weak flame. Our stomachs squeezed air out and filled up again. Bellies puffed out and contracted, puffed out and contracted.

On my ninth or tenth round of kapalabhati, I got dizzy. I also got nauseous. My pumping stomach ached like I had eaten too much rich food.

The fast exhale floated right up to my head, and my vision blurred behind closed eyelids. The teacher gave us permission to slow down or pause if needed. But I forced myself to keep going. I acknowledged the dizziness and the nausea, and welcomed them both into the breath practice. I imagined how good I would feel when we finished, so I continued despite my uncomfortable sensations. After two minutes, my dizziness shifted to an ethereal lightness. The nausea moved into my shoulder blades and created a dull tingling in my upper back and limbs. I relaxed my shoulders down and away from my ears and continued to breathe. I wiggled my toes and let the tension leave from my legs. The fast breath pulsed like warm coals in my belly.

Then, a dramatic shift happened. In the middle of an exhale, I felt my chest expand and my shoulders sink even lower into my back. Like a runner who finds her stride, in kapalabhati, I caught wind. I stopped resisting and flowed with the breath, rather than forcing it.

At the end of the pranayama, our instructor told us to take deep, slow inhales as we relaxed back into normal breathing. I filled my lungs with air and let the inhale travel liquidly down and throughout my abdomen. When I exhaled, my scalp tingled. Energy swirled around the room as the group's breaths, now stoked and fluttering easily in the air, mingled and eventually dissipated throughout the space.

We continued kapalabhati at the beginning of each class for the remainder of the semester. It never got easier for me, but I knew when to recognize the tightness right before the crest. If I breathed a little longer and pushed through the rising heat, I would reach the peak and ride the breath smoothly downhill to experience sweet coasting at the end. This was my favorite part—when the breath ended, the billows relaxed, and we sat in silence to allow the dust to settle.

I asked our instructor about the dizziness and nausea, and she explained that pranayamas like kapalabhati churn a lot of things up, like a rake that dredges the bottom of a lake to clean out debris and garbage. Churning is dirty at first, and the swirling can be physically uncomfortable. I walked out of class and wondered, What's being churned up in me?

One morning, while searching for my class binder, I found an old catalog announcing a yoga teacher-training program in Massachusetts. Kripalu. My heart floated upward in my chest when I read the name. My mom had given me the magazine years before when I was in high school. Every once in a while, the front cover with orange letters, tall evergreen trees, and the pointed tips of the Berkshire Mountains would grab my attention. I stopped what I was doing and allowed myself to flip through the pages, imagining what it would be like to enter a career in yoga. My soul felt temporarily at ease, my nervous mind settled down, and my worries about money and my future stood still.

When the tuition for yoga certification leapt out at me, I tucked the gentle whispers from my soul back into my body. I tuned my heart out and reminded myself that yoga is not a career; it is a pastime, and just because I enjoy it, who am I to pursue an ancient spiritual practice as my vocation? Still, I did not completely dismiss the idea, which is why the wrinkled, worn-out pages came with me everywhere. Maybe some day. I slid the catalog back into my bookshelf and grabbed my backpack for school.

I didn't know about yoga philosophy at the time, but the catalog was pointing me to my dharma. Dharma is our soul's purpose, and the path that leads us to our purpose is just as important as the destination. Dharma teaches us to listen to our own heart.

I stayed course and graduated with my bachelor's degree. I met my future husband, David, at a bar during my second semester of grad school. The Badgers were playing in the Sweet Sixteen Tournament, and the bar was nearly at capacity when my friends and I greeted the bouncer and flirtatiously begged to be let in. With no place to sit and barely space to move, a man offered his table as a spot for us to set down our drinks and our bags.

It worked. I talked to David all night, and to the disdain of my roommate, we saw each other every day in a row for four straight months after that. David was six years older than me, which felt safe and inviting because I thought it meant he was mature. We fell in love. I took a good job right after graduation teaching English at an art college in Chicago. Everything fell into place, I thought, so it had to be the right path.

SAVASANA

The siren from a fire engine screamed, and I lay quietly in savasana (corpse pose). As the sound of the engine faded down the road, my breathing finally found a quiet rhythm, and I forgot that I was in a crowded gym in downtown Chicago. Despite being adjunct faculty at a university and having no money, I had somehow paid for a membership at the trendy Cheetah Gym, which was within walking distance of my apartment. The daily yoga classes were filled with young men and women, all of us eager to sculpt our bodies and take a break from our lives. Most of us were just out of school, working a first job or bartending because it paid well. We didn't have a plan; we were in transition, and even a random trip to the gym could lead to a date or an exhilarating life-changing opportunity. There was freedom in the fact that we didn't have to have everything figured out, not in our twenties, not while we only had ourselves—living month to month—to worry about. Now I had David, who took some of the pressure off my unknown future and made it easier for me to live in the moment.

As we lay on our backs, the instructor reminded us to leave our stresses and doubts outside the studio and give ourselves a break during this final resting pose. My eyes were closed. My tongue gripped the roof of my mouth, so I let it drop heavily away, and my jaw relaxed. Blenders hummed from the juice bar right outside the room and filled in the clanging, uneven sounds of weights and machines in the busy gym. I heard the steady pattern of runners' feet on the soft rubber track upstairs.

I came back to a still, quiet mind. A soft, purple glow hovered near my forehead, and I realized I was squeezing my eyes too tightly. I loosened them, and my entire face instinctively relaxed in response.

A few minutes into savasana, I heard children giggling, slow and distant. Then the laughter sped up and their rhythm got closer together. I heard the laughter running upstairs above me or maybe in circles all around me, loud and melodic. The children, whoever they were, were playing and having fun. *But where were they? Was I hearing right?*

I came back to my forehead and ignored the young giggles. I felt like I was trying to wake myself up from a dream in order to focus on savasana, my mat, and the gym. But the children's laughter didn't stop, and now I heard their little feet pattering on the floor somewhere in the building. *Maybe someone brought their kids to the gym?* But the laughter seemed to be coming from right inside my head and not from within the building at all. Tiny voices danced and smiled. They laughed musically and without a worry or care. One seemed to be a boy and one a girl. But I felt crazy imagining what they looked like because that made them real.

When the instructor announced that it was time to move ourselves out of savasana, I eagerly opened my eyes and wiggled my fingers and toes. Class ended, and I exited the heavy glass doors of the dimly lit yoga studio and stepped into the glaring, brightly lit gym. Exercise machines lined every inch of the black, padded floor, and attractive young people ran in place on buzzing treadmills. Brightly colored tennis shoes flashed in my eyesight, and I scanned the room for any children present. A man at the bench press sweated through his thin gray t-shirt, and I could see his firm, defined muscles even through the fabric. A woman in a hot pink sports bra and matching neon sneakers climbed a stair stepper nearby. Her hair was pulled back neatly into a low bun, and she watched a cooking show on the built-in TV. I walked through the space in my leggings and flip-flops, my yoga mat rolled up tightly under my arm, careful not to bump into anyone. But I couldn't find any children.

Back at our apartment, I told my roommate Cait what happened. Cait believed strongly in dreams, intuition, and past lives as clues to our current reality. Since we were young, she had always loved practicing her psychic abilities on me.

Cait and I had been friends since the seventh grade when I moved to a new school mid-year. Cait saw me at the drinking fountain on my first day, and three days later we announced to everyone that we were best friends. At sleepovers, I sat cross-legged with my eyes closed, and seated across from me, Cait ran me through a body scan to relax every limb and every cell. She told me to focus on nothing but to stay present with her. During our readings, Cait saw all sorts of things about my past that I had never told her. She knew about my grandfather who died when I was a baby. She described the aunt who helped raise me. Cait cried often during our readings, as if she had opened a portal to my buried secrets and misplaced pain, maybe the collective pain of all thirteen-year-old girls caught in a world between adolescence and womanhood. When we sat across from each other in trust and in silence, the sadness that seeped out brought tears to both our eyes, even if we didn't understand why.

At fifteen, Cait and I had our first drink. The sickeningly sweet rum and coke we made from her parents' liquor cabinet left my tongue fuzzy and my throat numb. Since her parents were to be home soon, I guzzled more than sipped, trying to get to the drunk sensation as quickly as possible. The lightening of my limbs, the warm liquid in my chest, and the dizziness in my head made so much disappear. I felt nothing and everything all at once. Snuggling on the couch with Cait, watching a funny movie under a blanket, ice clanking in my glass was like being in a padded room with just the right amount of medicine. I was deliriously protected from any fear and any pain the world had brought upon me.

When I got back from yoga, Cait was fascinated by my dreamlike yet awake experience during savasana. She believed that visions and sensations in our body during meditation helped us to learn more about who we are and why we think and behave the way we do today.

I tried to latch on to Cait's enthusiasm about what the children meant. Were they my children? Were they from another life, or did they point to something in my future? Cait thought the children could be me, my own inner child trying to get my attention by running and laughing in circles inside my head.

I went to bed that night and could still hear their giggling.

THREE

Asteya : Nonstealing

"Oh, honey, of course it hurts! Beauty is pain. But
you don't want to look like a troll, do you?"

—Libba Bray

The third yama is asteya, which means "nonstealing." Like all yamas,
we apply the practice of non-stealing to others along with ourself.
From a young age, we learn to hide behind a mask or a role in order to
glean approval and acceptance from others. It works, so we continue
to wear the veil of someone we are not. We look outward and trust
others to tell us what is best for us instead of trusting ourself. We deny
our uniqueness, thinking it makes us separate. We shield ourselves
from the pain of not fitting in. We keep secrets and don more masks.
We falsely believe that marriage, the perfect dress, and the perfect
partner will fulfill us, even if we have not yet accepted ourself.

In yoga we're taught to trust the pose and to witness our body in order
to gain awareness of who we really are. We honor ourself by gently
coaxing an extra breath, a little more length, and a compassionate
letting go. After a lifetime of stealing from ourself, we slowly learn
that trust in our own heart might be possible.

KAPOTASANA

CAN'T BREATHE. I'M FOLDED COMPLETELY OVER MY RIGHT LEG IN
kapotasana (pigeon pose). My left leg stretches out behind me, my
arms reach forward, and I tent my fingers in order to relieve some of
the pressure in my abdomen. I relax my torso and loosen my hips, and
the weight of my body lays even heavier over my front leg. The crunched
position of my torso restricts the amount of air entering my belly and
lungs. The instructor says we will stay like this for eight minutes and
that we should keep breathing.

Kapotasana is my least favorite yoga pose. Others in the class seem easily and gracefully draped over their front legs, arms stretched forward, soaking in all the healing and cleansing benefits of the hip opener. The ground supports them comfortably as they lean completely into the pose. I unclench my jaw and remain hovering six inches above my mat.

After several minutes in the pose, I come up to balance awkwardly on my forearms, because my right hip has tensed up under my body weight. I inhale, then exhale deeply and notice I am gripping my right thigh along with all of my teeth.

Our yoga instructor paces quietly through the room. She pauses at the woman folded next to me in pigeon and squats down behind her. She applies gentle pressure to her hips with her hands and invites the woman to inhale and exhale fully. The instructor does the same, so both women breathe in sync, one inhale mirroring and giving permission to the other. Their exhales rhythmically release like leaves blowing steadily across a sidewalk.

The instructor gets up and arrives near me. She places her hands on my lower back and reminds the class: "If the pose is challenging for you, don't push, just observe."

She inhales behind me. I follow her breath with my own and fill my belly with air. Our breaths exhale together, and I am shocked that my hips move closer to the ground. The instructor does not press down on my back with her hands, but their warmth invites me to stay after the exhale, which is when I sink a little more deeply.

Patient and encouraging, our instructor's voice is almost a whisper. "One more inhale and we will slowly, very slowly push ourselves up and come to a seated position."

Before her words have finished, I lurch my torso upright and feel blood rush fuzzily into my head. I release my front leg from its bent position and stretch it out in front of me, which causes my entire ankle to tingle. I bring my back leg around to meet the other and playfully wiggle all ten of my toes. I lean back on my hands, take a deep breath, and arch backward. I watch my chest rise visibly with each inhale.

"Trust what your body is asking for. Trust your body. Trust YOURSELF." Our instructor's words echoed in my head as the dizziness settled, and I continued to breathe. "It's too tight," I told the seamstress. "I'm having trouble taking in a full breath." The wedding was a month away, and my custom-made Amsale gown had arrived and was ready to try on. David proposed the morning before New Year's Eve while I was still asleep in bed, hungover and tired from our antics the night before. I woke to him carrying a wobbly tray in my direction, the tall glass vase that held one rose nearly tipping over when he set it down on the bed. I sat up and looked at the plate of French toast and carefully laid orange slices and then at the black velvety box that sat next to the plate, open to reveal a large chunk of diamond raised above a narrow silver band.

"Yes!" I let David ask the question but only out of curiosity and politeness. I couldn't wait to say yes, start planning the wedding, and never have to worry about being alone again. We drank champagne continuously from that morning through New Year's Day.

I entered the department store on Michigan Avenue and wound my way up the shiny escalator to the seventh floor. I walked to the back of the room and took the special elevator to the eighth floor, the bridal showroom.

The elevator doors opened, and I stepped into a brightly lit white room. Glass tables displayed white flowers that sprang up out of clear vases. A curved, ivory sofa held an assortment of soft, plush pillows, and small, fuzzy ottomans hung out nearby. Magazines with white-teethed brides smiling broadly in white gowns on their covers were fanned intentionally on top of a low glass coffee table.

Janet, my consultant and seamstress, greeted me excitedly at the elevator door and pulled me in close. "It's here!" She harshly whispered as if my dress was a celebrity who had just arrived on the red carpet. Janet eyed me and tilted her head down the length of my body. I followed her gaze that landed on my frayed bell-bottom hems and scuffed sneakers. "Great!" I looked up and responded casually as Janet grabbed my hand to pull me hurriedly to the other side of the room.

We stopped at a line of three mirrors, two angled inward to create a half-ring. The beautiful gown was hanging there all on its own. I hardly wanted to ruin it by placing a body inside.

"Let's get you in this dress!" Janet exclaimed, a little too anxiously. I sensed that my body was supposed to fit the dress and not the other way around.

Janet brought out a small step stool and reached up to grab the hanger from the top of the mirror. She gently folded the top of the dress over one arm and cradled the heavy skirt with the other. She handed the garment to me like it was a delicate baby while directing her gaze toward a white door that signified where I was to change.

I came out of the dressing room with the long train dragging annoyingly behind me. The undone back hung wide open, so I awkwardly held up the front with both hands on my chest as I walked out to the pedestal and full-length mirrors. Janet turned my body around and began yanking the ties of the corset to lace up the back of the dress. I instinctively sucked in my breath and moved my hands onto my hips to stabilize myself.

"Inhale and then blow everything out," Janet instructed as she continued lacing up the corset. My ribcage drew in more tightly with each pull, and I wanted something to hold onto, but there was nothing, so I pressed my hands together in prayer pose at my heart and slowly lowered my chin as Janet finished tying up the back. After requesting one more exhale and clasping the final hook, Janet busied herself with the long train, arranging it around me in a contrived swirl. I lowered my hands to my sides and looked up to see my reflection in the mirror—the dress was beautiful. The fabric glistened under the soft lighting, and where it gathered at my waist, it created a perfect curve, like the shape had been cut out using the fin of a dolphin.

I lifted my gaze to see my face. My wind-blown hair from my walk to the El Train snuck rebelliously out from my low ponytail, and I hadn't put on enough makeup. I wore dangly plastic earrings, which looked fine with my jeans and t-shirt, but they appeared silly next to the elegant, sophisticated gown.

I felt cut in half...and like an impostor.

A mother and daughter who were visiting the bridal suite for the first time walked by me and stopped. The mother lifted her dark sunglasses off her face and dug into her oversized bag for their case. Her pointy high heels poked out neatly from the tailored hem of her tan pants, and her crisp, white blouse gleamed like my dress under the overhead lights. Her daughter was dressed similarly, except her high-heeled shoes were bright pink, and she was wearing designer denim instead of slacks.

"Oh, that is just beautiful!" the mother admired. "Who is the designer?" She nudged her daughter and commented on the mermaid style of my skirt. "Maybe you would like something like that?" Her daughter nodded and commented as if she might agree, but I couldn't actually hear what she said. They walked over to the mirrored silver desk and checked in for their appointment. The woman behind the desk took their coats and handed them each a sparkling glass of champagne.

I turned back to my reflection. "It's too tight," I repeated to Janet. "Can we loosen it here?" I pointed to my sides and my back where the corset pinched at my skin and shrank my ribcage. If I moved a certain way, the skin of my back smushed deceivingly over the wired edges of the bodice and made me look too big for the dress.

"Oh, your body will get used to the corset." Janet explained. "Right now your ribs feel tight, but once they are in there for a bit, they will relax all on their own."

Fine, I thought. I'd be careful about what I'd eat the next few weeks. Janet now worked below me, fluffing and rolling the hem of the dress in order to get the right length above my shoes. She asked about the neckline and if I'd rather have it dip down in the center, like a heart. I felt dizzy from not eating yet that day and having misjudged the time the fitting would take.

"It's great the way it is," I said. "I like the straight edge. Hearts are for little girls."

Janet paused, eyes still fixed at the neckline of the dress. She tilted her head to the side, the same way she did when she looked me up and down when I stepped off the elevator. If she disapproved of my choice, she made a note on her clipboard anyway.

"OK!" Janet chirped. "Now a very important part: How are you going to get out of this dress?" I had no idea the undoing was so involved, but I stepped out of the high-heeled shoes I was wearing and listened to Janet explain that a friend would have to undo everything in the back.

"I'm sure we can figure it out," I said, walking eagerly off the round platform and toward the changing room.

Janet dropped her pen and clipboard on the floor and grabbed me at the back of the dress. Her fingers swiftly released the top metal clasp, and my ribcage immediately puffed open, the freedom to breathe stopping me mid-stride. I continued moving toward the changing room, and once inside, I pulled on the tie that held the bow in place. I felt more relief as the laces naturally loosened and unraveled. Without following Janet's clear instructions, I squirmed my way out of the corset and eventually pulled the dress enough below my hips to step out.

Back in my regular clothes, I tucked the loose strands of hair behind my ear and left the dress hanging from the small hook behind the door. Janet folded her hands together over mine as I waited for the elevator to arrive.

"Four weeks!" she reminded me. "Whatever you do, don't let anything change on that gorgeous body in four weeks!"

FOUR

Bramacharya : Nonexcess

"Attachment is that which follows identification with pleasurable experiences. Aversion is that which follows identification with painful experiences."

—Sri Swami Satchidananda,
The Yoga Sutras of Patanjali, Book 2, Verses 8 and 9

The fourth yama is bramacharya, which means "nonexcess." Brahmacharya also translates to "walking with God." We continually acknowledge the sacredness of all our actions. We practice moderation in relationships, food and drink, material possessions, and any excesses, including addictions and our own emotions. We seek balance and the middle way.

Rather than crave the highest high, like a drink or a person, the practice of bramacharya is to remain steady and unnerved like a tree. There is no excessive high and also no coming down. The practice of bramacharya might sound boring and no fun, but like all the yamas, its purpose is to live by our character and not at the whim of external people or circumstance. Practicing bramacharya does not have to mean never indulging or never having fun; it means not becoming overly attached to pleasure and expecting it to be constant.

Another translation of this yama is "right use of energy." Bramacharya is a way to remain present instead of jumping ship when discomfort arrives. We can direct our energy away from something external that will bring temporary relief and toward an internal solution, a healing that can occur despite heartache or tragedy. Internal healing will be permanent and transformative.

ESCAPE

A FEW WEEKS BEFORE MY WEDDING DAY I MET SOME GIRLFRIENDS OUT in Chicago. It was July, and the city stayed hot and awake late into the night. David wanted to stay in, and I somewhat resented the fact that he was so disciplined about his weeknight routine. I always wanted to have fun. I craved a drink every night and a reason to go out. Chicago didn't care what day or time it was; there was always a place for those who wanted to escape. Staying in suffocated me. Without the people, the entertainment, and the alcohol, my body immediately erupted in anxiety. I felt alone, even with David right next to me.

I wore my favorite white blouse and sat confidently at the bar. The cute bartender flirted with me and my friends, and I flashed my engagement ring at him while drinking the free shots. Around 1:00 a.m., I left to go home. I hailed a cab outside the bar next to several other patrons doing the same, like I had done hundreds of times while living in the city. A cab was much safer than the bus or the El at night.

When my cab approached, I hopped in the front seat, shut the door, and pulled the seatbelt across my chest. I gave the driver David's address, and he asked me if the radio station he had on was OK.

"Fine," I said and continued looking out the window as he drove away from the bar, away from the people, and down the road toward home.

I don't remember if we had any conversation. I don't remember if I invited him to touch me. The next thing I remember was being completely reclined in the front seat of the cab with the driver on top of me. He kissed my neck and pulled on my head. His groin plunged repeatedly into mine. His hand groped at my bare breasts under my blouse, and he moaned desperately into my hair. The underwire of my bra dug painfully into my skin as his hands maneuvered underneath it. His weight and his thrusting on top of my body made my feet go numb and the rest of my legs tingle. My entire body throbbed. My arms felt limp and far away.

When I turned my face to the side and looked out the passenger seat window, I saw dark streets and tall gray buildings, nothing like my neighborhood. Where was I? Why was my seat reclined, and why was my cab driver on top of me? What was happening?

A jolting panic alerted my body into motion, and I pressed my palms firmly into the stranger's chest. My voice arrived and I began screaming. "Get off me! Get off!"

I kicked my legs and frantically slapped my hands into his chest and neck. Then I shoved, once and hard, and the man finally rolled his body off of mine. I found the door handle, flung open the door, and lurched my body out of the cab. I ran down the sidewalk, looking at buildings I didn't recognize, having no idea where I was in Chicago. I called David first, slowing to a jog and finding my phone at the bottom of my shoulder bag, but he didn't answer. Next I called our friend Scott. Scott answered right away and gave me simple instructions. He told me to stay on the phone as I did what he said.

"Molly, are you still there?" Scott kept repeating.

"Yes, yes, I'm here." But I wasn't, not really.

Scott's car pulled into the brightly lit gas station parking lot. The overhead lights exposed everything at night: my smudged makeup, my unbuttoned shirt. I ducked my head and crawled into the front seat of Scott's car. He asked me a bunch of questions, but I just wanted to get home to David.

Scott was crying and visibly shaken. He told me I hadn't sounded like myself on the phone; it was my voice, but something was missing. He said it was like talking to a ghost. I'd never felt so ghost-like, as if I was floating above everything and everyone while the night life of Chicago happened below me. I didn't remember how I got to the gas station from the dark sidewalk. I didn't remember how the cab driver convinced me to not go straight home.

We pulled up to the three-story brick building on a quiet street, and I thanked Scott for the ride. I moved to exit the car and told him I would be fine.

I used the key David had given me shortly after we started dating and unlocked the door. I walked down the long hallway to his bedroom. I stood helplessly in the doorway and couldn't stop staring at his back as he slept. I wondered if I had to wake him at all. Maybe I was making too big a deal over what just happened. Maybe I could keep it all to myself, and no one would ever have to know. I quietly crawled in to bed next to him and willed myself to fall asleep. Maybe upon waking, it all would seem like a dream.

"David," I eventually whispered hoarsely. I touched his right shoulder, which rose and fell as he slept; I wiggled it back and forth with my fingers. "David . . ." I wondered if he could smell the cab driver on me. I could smell everything—the driver, the cheap beer, the free shots, the fluorescent blue waterfall that splashed behind the bar where my girlfriends and I had taken a photo right before I left.

"Hey, did you have fun with the girls?" David finally woke up in reaction to me shaking his shoulder.

I told him we were in Lincoln Park at a bar and that I took a cab home by myself because everyone else wanted to stay. When I got in the cab, I sat in the front seat. I probably made some small talk. Why hadn't he taken me home?

David sleepily rubbed his eyes and yawned.

"Wait, what happened?" David's words were slow and spaced further apart than usual.

I spoke, but I couldn't remember important details. I remembered the damp sidewalk under my shoes as I ran. I remembered standing under a hot white light at the gas station, feeling completely exposed. My blouse—I remembered I had on my favorite white blouse.

My words and my rendition were confusing and circular, and none of my story made any sense. I didn't come out and bluntly say, *My cab driver tried to rape me.*

David scratched his head and looked at the clock, which said 3:38 a.m.

I continued trying to explain everything in chronological order. "Then I ran. I don't remember getting out of the cab, only running. I tried calling, but you didn't answer. Scott answered, and somehow he got me to meet him at a gas station. And now I'm here."

David stared at me.

"My God. Are you OK?" David's brain registered some parts of what I was saying, and he leaned in to give me a hug. His arms were warm and heavy like a heated blanket around my quivering shoulders.

He pulled away and looked at me. "Molly, you have to be more careful! You shouldn't have gone out alone so late. You shouldn't have gotten so drunk."

David's hair stuck up on the right side of his scalp, a result of sleeping on his cowlick. Moonlight streamed brightly through the window next to the bed and illuminated his left cheek in a bluish, shadowy glow. Some young people walked loudly down the alley outside the barred first-floor window; they laughed and screamed as they stumbled home from the bar. I looked back at David's eyes—dark, but not glaring, not angry. But I could see he was frustrated, and I wondered why I was waking him up with my own problems. David had to work early in the morning, and at this point, we were only a few hours away from the alarm going off. I was obviously fine because here I was.

"You're OK. You're home now." David seemed to read my mind.

As he continued staring at me, a burning ignited on the back of my neck that I hadn't felt before. Like dried tinder dropped into a hot flame, the fire took hold at the top of my spine and spread quickly across my shoulders and up my scalp.

David said we'd talk about it more the next day. He rubbed his eyes and rolled over to go back to sleep. He was glad I was home safe.

I laid down next to him and pulled the covers up to my chest. I stared at the ceiling from my back with my eyes wide open. I focused on my legs. My pelvis tingled and twitched as I remembered the man's relentless pressing and thrusting. My jeans had rubbed against my inner thighs, and my skin felt chapped and raw inside my sweatpants. I moved my focus to my vagina and tried to sense if it had been penetrated. I reached down and touched the tender skin. I felt each part and crevice in order to assess how deeply I had been violated. My hands moved up my torso to my breasts, and I could smell the man's ashy breath on my neck. I rolled over to face David's back, and I stared at it as I lay awake all night long.

This burning at the base of my neck was shame. Not guilt, not like forgetting someone's birthday or lying about who I was with. This was deep dark shame, something I couldn't apologize for and couldn't make better, even though it was somehow my fault. With this thought, along with the burning, something split open inside me and made a crack for darkness to settle in.

I remembered going out with my friends that night and feeling the need to completely let go. But really, it was the numbing I yearned for, not the release like we experience with a breath or a short meditation. Rather than seeking, I wanted to forget myself. I wanted to disappear inside the shots and beneath the thumping music. The low point after the assault reminded me of the high I experienced while at the bar—a forgetting, but also a betrayal of self. I wanted to be no one, and several drinks swiftly did the trick.

A week later I didn't feel any better. So I googled a therapist near the college where I taught. I walked the four blocks from work to the sleek black high-rise and pushed the button in the elevator for the floor I had scribbled down on a Post-it. Her office smelled of balsamic vinegar and salty tuna fish, and the acidic scents tickled the inside of my nose before making my mouth water. Once again, I hadn't eaten that day.

The therapist, who was about my age, apologized and told me she was just finishing lunch. I sat down on the oversized love seat that was squished next to the only window in the cramped downtown office. She pulled a straight chair around from behind her desk and sat upright in front of me. She asked why I was there.

So I rambled through the entire assault, and at the end I said, "I know I am lucky. I know I have a good life. Maybe this all happened to remind me to be grateful for the life I am about to have—my fiancé, my family, my career."

I was weeks away from marrying David. And there was no reason to put a wrench in my happy feelings or anyone else's. I didn't have to stop planning my wedding. David wasn't mad at me for getting drunk and hopping in a cab. He still wanted to marry me. In fact, he said what the cab driver did wasn't my fault. I had so much good going on in my life and a lot to be grateful for. I didn't have to let this break me. I didn't have to not get married. I didn't have to stop the rest of my life. I didn't have to stop anything.

The therapist let me talk most of our session, and at the end, she didn't correct me or urge me in any way. She didn't offer advice, only some kind words of understanding. When our time was up, she mentioned payment, so I pulled out my checkbook and wrote her a check for $150. My stomach rolled over; I would have to be very careful with spending this month. As I handed her the check, she said, "Good luck, Meghan. Have a wonderful wedding!"

I got in the elevator and waited for the door to close before allowing my tears to fall. The stinging behind my eyes had chastised me all the way down the hallway. Why didn't you correct her? She didn't even know your fucking name, and you just handed over your money to be polite. She didn't even help you. Do you care more about her feelings than your own?

I walked as quickly as possible back to my office as if running from another assault, another time I had been used, and another betrayal of my trust. I decided I couldn't trust anyone. I decided I would singlehandedly carry the assault because I was strong enough, and it was mine to carry.

And so I do, forever.

FIVE

Aparigraha : Ungrasping

"I took a deep breath and listened to the old
brag of my heart: I am, I am, I am."

—Sylvia Plath

The fifth yama is aparigraha, which means "ungrasping." The practice of letting go is one of the most elusive and challenging for our emotional self. What we want, we reach for. When we feel something leaving, we grab on more tightly, too afraid to let go. Losing something familiar becomes more important than whether or not we even want it anymore.

The familiar may be unhealthy, abusive, or harmful, but it is comfortable, and so we stay. We stay in unhealthy relationships. We stay in unfulfilling jobs. We stay in false thoughts and made-up stories in our heads. We stay in our beliefs and our habits. Part of personal growth is having the willingness to let go. We release expectation. We let go of our fear of failure or what people might think. We release the heavy burden of fitting in. The practice of aparigraha leads to less striving, less grasping, and more peace.

SAMSKARA

MANY YEARS LATER, IN OUR HOUSE OUTSIDE OF CHICAGO, NOW married and with two children, I wake up, startled, from a dream. I crack open my eyes and slowly let the shadow-light of night in. David's back faces me, as usual, as he sleeps calmly on his left side. His head lays sunken into the pillow as if his skull is temporarily detached from his spine. With each inhale, his right shoulder inches slightly upward then falls back down. The audible rumbling inside his nose and throat alerts me to his deep state of sleep. I am jealous because he appears peacefully at rest and oblivious while I remain wide awake.

An unassuming yet palpable wave of terror washes over me. My stomach tightens and a thick lump of clay jumps into my throat. I can sense someone else's lips on his. He lies in bed with his broad back to mine, securing a walled-off, impenetrable position, and I know I have lost him. A small circle of heat forms on the back of my neck like someone has placed a hot coal there, and the burning sensation travels outward to my shoulders and onto my scalp. I immediately brush the nape of my neck with my right hand and try to alleviate the heat.

My husband is in love—with another woman.

The truth feels unbelievable to me because I have been his for so long. Like a perfectly dressed doll displayed on a pedestal, I've stood there. And who am I once I tumble from that position? No longer the favorite one?

I immediately feel abandoned and blame myself for having acted badly. This is my fault. *You've really done it this time, Molly.*

Lately, I have asked David too many annoying questions. But I can't help impose when I experience his face. He bites on his lower lip, his eyes always flipped downward, and I can see the dancing fire that escapes his gaze. When I notice his expressions, I ask meekly, "Are you mad? Have I done something to upset you?" I wait for a hug or grin of reassurance.

Before my question is all the way out, he shakes his head emphatically—NO—and his eyes squeeze more tightly together. His lips curl around his teeth, and he answers back: "Stop asking me that! I'm fine. This is just who I am."

Our drinking has led each of us to disaster on several occasions, and I start to wonder if it's any fun anymore. We seem to keep bailing one another out, at different times, like we are on two separate roller coaster tracks with alternating highs and lows. David will get injured or arrested while I am functional and coasting. Then I will be the one who needs help out of a free fall, like the time I passed out on the couch, and my own children couldn't wake me up. Yet none of the consequences deter us. Once the dust settles, we head straight back to the poison, pouring drinks and expecting this time to be different.

I squish my head further into my pillow and try to go back to sleep, but I can't stop staring at my husband's back. Wondering if he is actually in love with someone else reveals so much of him that I haven't allowed myself to see until now—and so much of me that I haven't seen, or haven't wanted to. I do not own this man. He is not mine, forever and ever, until death do us part.

We sleep in our suburban house, many miles away from the city of Chicago where we met. Chicago is where David and I began our life—where we dated, moved in together, and brought our babies home. We were the last of our friends to leave the city for family life. We refused and resisted the common path to a larger, more convenient home in the suburbs. I miss Chicago, and I sense David does too. The dirt and grit of the city stick to me, and I have trouble relating to the flower beds and pleasant neighbors in small-town Wisconsin.

I stare at David's shoulder still moving up and down in our bed. The uneasy feeling in my stomach pulls. A cool wind rushes through the open window, fanning out the sheer curtain near our bed, and the wildfire at my neck erupts into flames.

Our bodies now warm from cat/cow, my yoga instructor Andrea tells us to lift our knees and complete three full breath cycles while in plank. I welcome the intensity. I welcome the burning sensation in my abdomen that provides temporary relief from the tingling anxiety at my neck and scalp. Finally, on an exhale, we lift our bodies up and back before we land comfortably in downward facing dog.

To every pose in yoga there is a counterpose, an opposite to bring balance. Like in life there is a price to pay for every action, a karmic pattern that repeats itself for every unhealed samskara. Samskara means "imprint" in Sanskrit and refers to mental paths left by our past, our experience, and our intentions. Past actions create psychological grooves that form our habits, our beliefs, and our personalities. Some samskaras are healthy, like taking a walk in nature when we feel anxiety. Samskaras can also be unhealthy, like using drugs or food as an escape anytime we feel triggered by an uncomfortable emotion. Repeated actions as a result of a belief form deep, often subconscious scars. We think we are acting out of logic and reason when in fact, the groove is so embedded in our psyche we don't have as much control over the action as we think.

When I was five years old, I climbed up on the weathered fence in my Grandma's front yard and sat on the railing. I perched myself on the side of my hip and crossed my legs—an imitation of a sexy, adult woman—like I was leaning on a city barstool rather than a country post. With one hand on the fence to keep my balance and the other holding a long, thin stick, I pretended to smoke a cigarette.

"Molly, what are you doing?" my aunt asked as she looked up from plunging tulip bulbs into the soil and pulling unwanted weeds out.

I exhaled pretend smoke from my stick and answered in a grown-up voice, enunciating every syllable. "When I grow up, I'm going to smoke cigarettes and drink martinis."

My aunt laughed and laughed, and I'd never seen her so taken by me. I felt important, feminine, and sexy.

The story behind a wound reveals the root of the samskara and is the entry point to healing. The problem with our psychological scars is that they may have been formed as a result of a long-ago experience that we no longer remember or from something we had no control over, like abuse, trauma, or simple misperception. Healing requires awareness, and without an understanding of our higher self, our habits become second nature; we perform them almost without choice. We cycle through the same behaviors over and over throughout our lives. Like an addiction, we repeat the same pain, dig deeply into the scar, and mindlessly traverse the same familiar groove. The deeper the original belief or intention that created the action, the harder it is to overcome that samskara and let go of the associated belief.

My imprint, the path I have traversed my entire life, is my intention to get people to like me and to approve. That's how I make sure I won't ever have to be alone. Looking good, feeling good, being good—this is why people like me. This is why people stay. If I always share a perfect smile and lend a funny joke, people will be happy. If I look the part, like the adult woman drinking in her wantonness and exhaling her flirtatious appeal, I will always be surrounded by people who won't want to leave me.

Sanskrit words have many definitions, so another translation of samskara is "rite of passage" or a "new path toward awakening." When we remove the layers of our conditioning and illuminate the scar, we can heal the samskara. In this way, the scar becomes a powerful symbol of our path and our overcoming. When we intentionally let go of old patterns, behaviors, beliefs that hide the truth, we free up our bodies and our brains to accept the new behavior and a new perspective. We intentionally decide to form a new groove; we rake a new line in the sand.

Still unable to sleep, I think back on the night with the cab driver in Chicago. I watch David's back carefully in our bed. His shoulders are broad and hard as he lays like a solid statue on his side—unlike me when I sleep; I am more like a Raggedy Ann doll tossed into the sheets, flat on my back, legs twisted around the comforter, and arms sprawled out above my head. My right cheek tilts to one side, and my wavy hair dangles off the edge of the pillow. David's muscular shoulders look ten feet tall next to me. Sometimes I try to wrap myself around him at night when I can't sleep, but my arms and my limbs strain in order to reach up and around him, which feels like holding on instead of being held.

I cling to David because I don't know what else to do when I feel him slipping away, especially at night when the loneliness envelops our room like a dense fog. If I could just squeeze him more tightly, maybe I'd feel the heaviness inside me lift.

Lying in bed, I remember the times I've sat across from David on the couch and watched him check his phone; he constantly moves it in and out of his back pocket. I think of the times he's left to go on a trip and the times I've called him while he is away and get his voicemail. I am always quick to assume it is me; I must be an ungrateful wife to be so jealous when my husband's job takes him away. He's working hard and earning money, and I am accusing him of cheating.

I am also jealous of his ability to sleep. David's world must be completely intact, which is why he sleeps so soundly.

I rub the back of my neck with my hands. I yank on the rubber band holding my ponytail and shake out my hair so there is less pulling at the nape of my neck. I touch the top of my head with one finger, and the crackling flames at my neck rush to my crown. I know there is an answer.

Looking back, I wonder: Maybe David was not intact. Maybe he was completely unaware and unavailable—for himself and for me.

Yoga creates space and pause so we can live in the question instead of the assumption or the desire for an answer. Breath and poses allow us access to more questions, which in turn address and pull back more layers of self. The deeper you go and the more you practice, the closer you get to your indestructible center, the parts you need to hear, and your truth.

I learn I am not crazy but rather aware, and the burning on my neck is an example of tapas, a Sanskrit word for "discipline," or "burning away impurities," also the third of the niyamas in Patanjali's Eight Limbs. I may have been extremely uncomfortable, my skin even on fire, but unlike my peaceful husband, this burning, nagging sensation forces me to keep searching, to stay on the path, and to keep asking important questions.

The next day I wake up alone. I remember hearing the garage door open and close around 4 a.m. when David left to go to the airport. I turn over inside the sheets and look at the clock—5:30 a.m. The boys will wake up soon, so I tip-toe downstairs to make coffee. I rub my neck with my hand as I run water to fill the coffee pot. I pour the water into the coffeemaker, which is already turned to "on" so the water puffs up loudly, exhaling steam like a coughing smoker. I grab a pink ceramic mug out of the cabinet and sit in my chair at the kitchen table to wait for the coffee to brew. I look out the window at our stone patio and the park just beyond. A woman walks her dog around the path that encircles a basketball court. I realize I am always in this chair. I sit in the exact same spot every morning and for every meal. Family photos of holidays and gatherings show me in this chair. My neck ignites with heat, and I remember my Grandma always sat in the same spot at her kitchen table, no matter the time of day. We could always expect to find her there, looking out the large picture window as we entered the fenced yard and trekked up the long sidewalk to her front door. After her husband died, my grandma had the same view for the last fifty years of her life.

I drop the boys off at school and go to yoga class. I hold my elbows with my hands and bend over my legs in rag doll pose. I give my body permission to hang, and then naturally, my torso begins to sway. While in rag doll, I welcome the pause, the dead-weight pull of gravity, and the opening up of the backs of my thighs. I enjoy the length and release in my lower back and imagine myself growing slightly taller. I welcome the heaviness of my skull as it dangles off the top of my spine. My neck feels relief from the incessant tingling while in this pose. The aroma of sage burning in the room mixed with the lavender oil I rubbed on my temples this morning opens my sinuses and evaporates lightly on my skin.

Andrea moves us into shoulder stand before we come down into savasana to end the class. Sarvangasana (shoulder stand) is one of my favorite yoga poses. An inversion, my legs and feet reach to the sky and hang upside down freely. My neck and shoulders remain immobile on the mat, the foundation that holds everything up.

I lift my hips as high as they will go. My butt sits heavily in my palms, and I inch up on my shoulders more so they can bear the weight. I move my hands to support my lower back, and my entire body stands inverted on top of my shoulders and upper back. My chin tucks all the way down, almost to touch my chest, which fully constricts my throat.

With nothing to do and unable to move my neck, I focus on my feet and toes floating toward the sky. I press my hands into my hips and lift them even higher, then remove one hand to fix my t-shirt, which has fallen toward my face to reveal my bare stomach. I grab the fabric and tuck it inside the waist of my sweat pants, then return my hand to my lower back and continue to hold the pose.

Andrea reminds us that shoulder stand can make people anxious or claustrophobic with so much weight being placed on the thyroid. But I don't mind the sensation of a closed throat. In fact, I am very comfortable here.

In savasana at the end of class, Andrea invites us to visit a friendly place from our past. "I am ... " she repeats rhythmically. "I am ... I am ... I am."

Lying on my back, I imagine myself being supported by the hill near our summer cottage. I brush the tips of grass across my palms and inhale the crisp, fall air. Birds play in the trees outside the glass doors of the studio, and the passing traffic sounds like the flowing creek from my past. The furnace clinks on, and the woman next to me coughs. Distracted, I reach up to scratch my eye, then quickly pull it back down and focus on my forehead, the grassy hill, and my eleven-year-old self. I see the purplish glow and my eyelids flutter. Andrea walks through the room and bends to touch each student's temple with oil. A voice speaks to me, the kind you know isn't really yours. The voice says, "I can. I am. I will." Tangerine and basil mingle inside my nostrils, both sweet and bright compared to the earthy sage smoking on the windowsill. A new scent from my past enters my nostrils: burning leaves that my father used to stoke on Sundays in the fall.

Finally outside of class, I get in the car and toss my mat onto the passenger seat. I sob over the steering wheel, the foreign tears streaking my face and landing in my lap. I have grown quite skilled at ignoring my emotions, pushing them down, and squeezing them tight until they have no place to breathe, no room in my unaccepting body. But this time I cannot deny the tears, and they rush out of me like the creek that travels obediently downhill to meet the reservoir, where it lands and disperses, finally able to merge with its home in open water.

The voice in our head is oddly loud. Yet we deny it or mistake it for a crazy lapse. But we know. Deep down we know something (someone) is speaking to us, and the words are not coming from our rational mind.

I can . . .

I hunch over the steering wheel and think, *I can't. Who am I to cry?*

I am . . .

The words pour into my mind like the tears onto my lap. *I am lonely. I am addicted. I am afraid.*

I will . . .

I will what?

I go home and write the words in large capital letters on the whiteboard in my office.

I CAN

I AM

I WILL

I know they are a message of hope from my soul and will reveal their meaning when I am ready.

PARIVRITTA TRIKONASANA : REVOLVED TRIANGLE POSE

PART II

The Five Niyamas

SACRED RITUALS THAT DEEPEN OUR PRACTICE

"The five points of Yama, together with the five points
of Niyama, remind us of the Ten Commandments
of the Christian and Jewish faiths, as well as
the ten virtues of Buddhism. In fact, there is no
religion without these moral or ethical codes."

—Sri Swami Satchidananda

SIX

Saucha : Purity

"You will never be more complete than you already are."

—Molly Chanson

Saucha is the first niyama and means purity or cleansing. To practice saucha, we cleanse the physical body and our environment. Every morning, we wash our face and brush our teeth. Many normal hygiene practices can be done with the intention of saucha. We cleanse in order to eliminate the junk that has collected. In our home, we declutter and make space.

We also observe saucha in terms of our emotional self; we unload what is heavy. We make space within ourselves for new habits and beliefs to form. We don't need to drag around the past because it prevents us from being present. We don't need to collect more people, possessions, or accomplishments to make us feel whole or complete. We are pure with the present moment when we accept ourself as we are. And we do the same for others, without expecting them to change in order to meet our demands. Purity does not mean perfection; it means acceptance of what is.

PARIVRITTA TRIKONASANA

I HATED THE PINK AND GREEN FLORAL WALLPAPER IN THE WOMEN'S locker room at the country club. Along with the painted white wicker furniture, I felt like I was visiting an old house from my childhood. A friend of my grandma always served us cookies and small glasses of juice when we visited. My brother, sister, and I sat on her floral furniture inside a screened-in porch. My legs dangled playfully off the edge of the tucked cushion as we ate and drank in order to relieve our boredom.

Twelve women were getting ready in this outdated locker room, and despite standing upright inside the corset of my dress, my weak knees and ankles felt as though they were dangling off the edge of a couch. It was my wedding day.

My bridesmaids busily checked and rechecked their lipstick and added extra pins to their hair. It had already rained, so my friend Jen used a blow dryer to remove the dark water marks splattered on her silk dress.

My cousin Taylor suggested we take a picture. I posed next to her in my long white veil and smiled as more of my friends and family pulled out their phones.

An usher poked his head inside. "I think we're almost ready. Five minutes?"

I nodded as a familiar knot squeezed in my stomach. I hadn't been nervous all day. I turned to my mom and said a little too loudly, "I think I might throw up."

"Are you sure? Do you want to do this?"

I was annoyed because my mom acted like I still had a choice; I didn't have to walk down the aisle. But to me, of course I did; it was too late.

I'd had my wedding dress on since that morning, but several hours later, before I was about to walk down the aisle, I still couldn't breathe properly inside the corset. I remembered Janet from the dress fitting telling me my ribcage would get used to the dress. I wondered what was wrong with me. Why couldn't I just go with the flow and get used to things like everyone else? The mother and daughter in the dress showroom smiled and salivated over all the ornate gowns. They clinked and sipped their afternoon glasses of champagne as they wandered casually through the bridal showroom. Their happiness made me feel out of place—like an impostor pretending to know about love—and I felt out of place in that locker room. Even on my wedding day, when everything was perfect, my body resisted this beautiful dress.

Despite my fluttering stomach, I reminded myself that this was all normal. It's OK to ignore your gut on your wedding day. You're supposed to be nervous. After all, marriage is the goal. There's no reason to be nervous when you're about to walk down the aisle and complete yourself. I wanted to be complete. I wanted to cross the threshold into marriage and not have to worry about anything ever again. No more dates, no more unfaithful boyfriends, no more dangling in the world all alone like the final leaf waiting to fall.

Every Sunday, as a girl, my family went to church. I sat in the long, hard pew and looked around at the congregation. On Sunday mornings, people were dressed up and meditative, but during the week, I witnessed greed, jealousy, selfishness, and drunken fights. I listened to the teachings of Jesus preached during the sermon but felt confused about how one achieves an ethical way of life. What does it mean to live like Jesus? Certainly, it doesn't mean going to church and hiding behind nice clothes. Could anyone really attain a spiritual existence?

When it was time, I walked confidently outside and to the beginning of the narrow, grassy walkway flanked by chairs. Ivory petals were strewn on stiff blades of grass that matched my soon-to-be husband David's boxy, white blazer.

My body was fighting for space to breathe, but I was in love with my dress. I endured the tightness because the dress was so beautiful. The fit, I was assured, was perfect. I chose the perfect dress.

I paused at the beginning of the aisle as I had been instructed and waited for the music to start. My ivory designer gown hugged tightly around my torso and hips, then widened just below my knees and cascaded impressively down, around, and behind me. Inside the gown, my waist and ribcage were tightly laced, which created a sensuous curve between my hips and bodice.

Around the corset, the gown's crisp, dewy fabric held its shape like a wet cast around my body. Silky layers gathered diagonally toward my right hip, where a silvery studded pin sparkled proudly in the August sunshine. Because of the adornment and the obvious attention to detail on the part of the designer, I didn't wear any other jewelry.

I allowed the dress to stand on its own. I was just a body, a prop for the dress's big reveal.

Revolved triangle pose is a standing balance as well as a twist. I try to breathe while in parivritta trikonasana (revolved triangle pose), but everything feels tight when I try. I focus on my legs and feet that press evenly on my mat. I twist my chest open to the sky and stack my shoulders one on top of the other. I want to touch the ground with my left hand because I think this will achieve the desired alignment. At least I can use my arm as leverage to twist my torso further into the pose. But when I touch the ground with my left hand, my heart and chest drop, and my shoulders curl inward.

My heart does not revolve but remains closed.

To adjust, I leave the security of my supporting hand. I lift my fingers slowly off the mat and return my hand to my hip. I use my obliques to lift my entire torso higher, more upright. In doing so, I allow more space for my torso to open, and my heart turns naturally toward the sky. I place my left hand on my left shin, instead of the ground, and everything shifts accordingly: my tailbone tucks under, my hips are square, my chest faces up and out. My tired knuckles turn pink again as blood flows freely, and all four points of my feet take over to ground my body to the mat.

I believed that once I got married, everything would fall into place. The ritual would take hold, and I would experience true love. I would be safe from abandonment and hurt. I would finally be free from groping men and unsolicited advances. My diamond ring would always be a protective barricade that prevented me from ever having to explain myself. But the perfect dress and the perfect wedding are only a symbol, not the foundation of a perfect marriage.

Like anything we seek outside ourselves, a pristine outer appearance cannot cure poor body image. A successful career and expensive car cannot eliminate low self-worth. As humans, we always want to work from the outside in. But when we practice the five niyamas, we engage in the deep inner work required to remove false stories, shed superficial layers, and question conditioned beliefs. In doing so, we can uncover truth.

When we live according to the five niyamas, we uncover pieces of ourselves that have been buried and lost. As our self-awareness grows, our contentment grows. We are happier, lighter, and free from stories and misperceptions. Maybe we are not free from pain, but we are free from judgment and association with that pain. The five niyamas are: **saucha:** purity; **santosha:** contentment; **tapas:** self-discipline; **svadhyaya:** self-study; and **isvara-pranidhana:** surrender to a higher power.

Janet from the dress fitting was sort of right. My ribcage let go of the tightness as the wedding ceremony progressed. My body got accustomed to the constriction from my dress, and by the time I recited my portion of the vows, I was not thinking about my body or the dress at all. I looked at David. It was his turn now. I watched his face and mouth through the thin veil of fabric that hung over my face. My mom bought my veil for me, which had a very expensive price tag considering it was only one long length of tulle hemmed with a white ribbon. The mesh softened David's skin and added a playfulness to his eyes.

When the pastor nodded, David slowly lifted my veil away and off my face. A whipping breeze took hold of the airy tulle attached at my bun and lifted the lightweight fabric into a long, impressive streak of white behind me, a remnant, like the exhaust left from a jet plane's wake. The photographers scrambled close and crouched to snap the shot. I slid a silver band onto David's left hand, and he did the same on my finger. I looked down at the ring on my left hand and back up at David. Our eyes met, and we were officially husband and wife.

When we arrived at the other end of the aisle, someone handed us each a glass of champagne as people lined up to congratulate us.

With his arm on my shoulder, a family friend said into my ear, "Did you hear what happened before you came out?"

"No, what?" I answered, smiling back, and taking too big a sip of my champagne.

"While David was standing at the altar, a boat drove by on the lake, and some guy yelled out 'DON'T DO IT!' Everyone laughed and laughed."

I smiled as he told me the story, but a hot tingling erupted on the back of my skull. The sting of society's messaging made me feel embarrassed; I felt like a silly girl playing dress-up. Women desire marriage and commitment; men do not. Still, I didn't understand the joke. I brushed off the incident by the time the next guest embraced me. I sank the anger deep inside my stomach where it swirled patiently with all my other resentments.

I inhale in revolved triangle pose, and my breath enters like a breeze fluttering between leaves on a tree. The air fills my ribcage and disperses through my kinked cells and organs. When the breath reaches my abdomen, it massages my intestines and brings queasiness to the lower left side of my belly button. I will the sick feeling away and continue to breathe. But the nausea continues, and I have a choice. I can ignore the sensation and push through. Or I can honor my gut and lift out of the ickiness to give my heart room to open and revolve—to evolve. The swirling is a gentle reminder that everything buried doesn't disappear. In revolved triangle pose, I learn that I can open more than I thought. In the unacknowledged spaces revealed by the twist, my suppressed voice surfaces and gently inquires: *What is it you want to say?*

SEVEN

Santosha : Contentment

"In giving birth to our babies, we may find that we
give birth to new possibilities within ourselves."

—Myla and Jon Kabat-Zinn

The second niyama is santosha and means "contentment." We
practice being content with life as it is in front of us. To practice
santosha does not mean we are happy all the time. Contentment in
yoga means to fully experience the moment, no matter how we label
it. Our expectations for things to look and feel a certain way keeps
us from our own center and peace. The only thing that is real is what
is happening right now. This moment is perfect not because it feels
good but because it is all there is. Santosha teaches that our own
contentment relies solely on our ability to accept things as they are,
our fears, our sadness, and the unknown.

GARUDASANA

SINCE THE FETAL MRI WOULD TAKE AT LEAST AN HOUR, I DECIDED TO
use the bathroom. While washing my hands, I noticed myself in the
mirror, still not comfortable with my own reflection. The thin hospital
gown given out at doctors' visits used to envelop me like a young child
trying on her dad's dress coat. But that day the small ties barely reached
one another across my pregnant belly. The pale blue, wrinkled fabric
jutted diagonally at the hem and draped down low in the back, almost
to my ankles, but hung much higher in the front.

My appearance reminded me of playing dress-up with my grandma's
silk scarves; my siblings, cousins, and I used to tie them across our
small hips and baggy Lee jeans as skirts or wrap them around our
heads and pretend we were gypsies. We'd read each other's fortunes
using the round glass balls from Sweden my grandma had decorating
her living room. Whimsical, colorful flowers were blown from a glass

pipe to decorate the inside of each perfectly round ball, so no two were exactly the same.

Glancing one more time in the mirror, I tucked some hair behind my ear and shuffled out of the bathroom in the non-slip socks the check-in nurse had given me to wear. My inadequacy and self-doubt at being a first-time mom matched my awkward reflection in the mirror. I donned the outfit, but the hemline looked slightly crooked.

Two weeks earlier, while lying on the examination table for fear I might faint, the nurse took yet another round of blood. I touched my stomach, mostly due to wanting to throw up, and reassured the baby it would be OK.

After drawing the last vial, the nurse propped me up on two pillows and told me the ultrasound technician would be right in. I had decided not to find out if we were having a boy or a girl; we wanted to be surprised. I just wanted to see the photos and take them home like so many I had seen decorating refrigerators and people's nurseries, grainy black-and-white images on a wobbly strip of shiny printer paper, an automatic white frame surrounding several black boxes. I wanted to know that every body part was accounted for and every cell was growing as it should be.

"If you don't want to know, look away."

The technician arrived and placed a large amount of cold clear jelly on my stomach. She pressed forcefully with a plastic wand connected to a computer screen with a cord. I ignored her advice and looked at the screen anyway, but I couldn't discern most of the shapes. I could see a clenched hand perched up by the baby's forehead and his or her feet with tiny, circular toes that looked like white pebbles drifting through a murky black ocean. The fuzzy baby parts appeared and disappeared, a black-and-white puzzle to me, as the technician continued to maneuver her wand and snap still shots from the keyboard.

Partway through the exam, the technician paused. She had just shown me all ten toes and two chubby hands, pursed full lips, and a little round nose. But then her chattiness subsided, and she nervously walked to the door. She left and told me to wait.

The doctor that the technician went to get opened the door and peered at the small computer screen frozen on a shot of the baby's skull. He removed his glasses and continued looking, clicking through more images.

"See that dark spot right there on the right?"

The doctor pointed to the round mass on the screen. I saw many dark spots, grainy and distorted, but I nodded anyway.

"That's not supposed to be there. It's an indication of fluid on the brain. Of course, it could be nothing and go away on its own. But we need to be sure."

Sure of what? I wondered.

Is something wrong with my baby?

As the doctor continued describing the dark spot, the words "fluid," "brain," and "options" floated anxiously about the room. Since I had opted to not find out the sex, he did not say "he" or "she," just "the baby."

I felt naive and blind-sided. This appointment was not just to find out the sex of my baby but to make sure nothing else was revealed. I wanted to pay attention to the doctor, but I couldn't take my eyes off the screen. When the baby moved inside my stomach, I watched in order to match the sensation with what the baby was doing. A sharp stretch in my skin was a heel pressing out. A faint bubble that felt like a shooting star was a hand circling. A tumbling waterfall that plunged deep into my stomach was the baby's entire body rolling over.

When the ultrasound was complete, the doctor suggested we do a fetal MRI at Children's Hospital in order to see more clearly what was going on in the baby's brain. They had an opening in two weeks. Two weeks. I would find out whether there was something wrong with my baby in two weeks.

In eagle pose I focus all of my attention on one leg. Like a tall bird, my weight presses down on my entire foot and five toes, and I pull up in my standing thigh. The rest of my body perches above, right knee raised, arms hanging at my sides, my head and shoulders nearly floating off the top of my body.

I bend my left knee and sit back, crossing my right leg over the left. Once my right foot is tucked snugly behind my calf, I straighten my upper body and tighten my core. I sink deeper into my supporting leg, and with my right leg crossed so securely over my left, my two legs become one; I'm like a heron who rests and roosts on one leg in order to conserve her energy. I sense my toes clinging too tightly to the mat, and their gripping effort is unproductive. I don't need to try so hard. Trusting, I lift each toe, give them space to wiggle, and place them, one by one, gently back on the mat.

Santosha teaches us to remain neutral and rooted in the present. A desired outcome—a marriage, a baby, a new job, a much-anticipated trip—will not bring contentment if we aren't already grateful for what is. The paradox of santosha, like the paradox of eagle pose, is that we must practice acceptance for where we are and release expectation in order to be fully present for whatever comes next.

For the next part of garudasana (eagle pose), I twist my arms up the same way I have wrapped my legs. I extend both arms out to the side, in a T. On a forceful exhale blown out of my mouth, I swing both arms in front of me and cross my left arm over the right. (In eagle, if the right leg crosses over the left, you cross the opposite arm on top, and vice versa.) I cross my elbows first, then forearms, and I continue to wind until my wrists cross and my palms touch. My arms twist together like two ropes in gym class. When fully wrapped around one another, I lift both arms up and keep my fingers pointed to the sky. I pull my elbows away from my chest and press upward. The backs of my shoulders stretch, and I feel my shoulder blades spread apart.

With my limbs completely braided together, wound up and clasped at the end by my fingers and toes, I am extremely stable and relieved. Normally, a stretch in my body is achieved by reaching out, extending a leg and leaning over, or raising my arms and curving them to one side. Conversely, eagle pose stretches my entire body through a paradoxical wrapping and twisting. Curling up actually lengthens muscles that don't otherwise pull this way.

I am twisted so tightly in garudasana I almost can't move. My limbs have surged together as one, which alerts me to breathe, and not unwind, not yet, not until the pose has taken effect.

I went back to work after the disturbing ultrasound and began to teach my afternoon class. As I taught, the possibility of there being something wrong with my baby sunk in. The printed, fuzzy black-and-white photos showing tiny feet and an angelic profile sat folded neatly in my backpack, ready to display proudly on my refrigerator.

Those fingers, toes, and profile were living inside my stomach. I could tell the baby's chin already looked like mine—small and pointed like a strawberry. The feet kicked and woke me up at night; sudden jabs prompted me to choose a different sleeping position. Arms reached almost through my skin and my blouse and had forced a few students to jump back as I leaned over their table to check their assignment. "Sorry," I always said, feeling the need to apologize for my rude, unruly stomach. But the moment was actually sacred, and the student always smiled because we both acknowledged the realness of it all.

The baby growing inside of me became apparent in my physical body, yet my identity blurred. I was so used to controlling my body and outer appearance, and pregnancy diminished that control. I wondered who I even was anymore. Was that girl before pregnancy real? And will she be back?

I drank Coca-Cola every day for the next two weeks, something I never gave myself permission to do while not pregnant. All my addictions—caffeine, wine, my body image—had been ripped from me, and the sugary, fizzy beverage in the red can was the only thing I had left. Taking a sip as I sat in my car, listening to loud music that the baby could feel and hear brought some relief. David was on edge, worried as much as I was and probably feeling even more helpless, less connected to me and the baby. Two weeks of waiting for a life-altering test result crippled our ability to have fun; the second we started to laugh or enjoy ourselves we felt we were ignoring reality. I felt like I couldn't move for fear of doing something wrong, but I also couldn't stop moving because I didn't want to be still with my thoughts.

My mind wanted to go there—thinking and guessing and falling apart. Just like in yoga, my thoughts tried to move me to anything outside of class, away from the pose. But when present, the reality is that there is nothing to fear, no imminent collapse, even when we tip and flail. So I held myself like I held the baby, like I hold a pose, with gentle reassurance, abiding presence, and deep breaths.

Two excruciating weeks later, I emerged from the bathroom of Children's Hospital in my ill-fitting gown and socks, ready, I thought, for the test.

The nurse poked her head out of a heavy wooden door and called my name. David and I followed her into a small, perfectly square room with nothing on the pale, barely blue walls.

"Are you claustrophobic?" the nurse with the clipboard asked. The room on the eighteenth floor had no windows and only a few chairs. The brown desk and hutch cabinet provided the only visual backdrop. The nurse's clipboard rested on her lap as we sat across from one another. I had no idea if I was claustrophobic; I'd never been enclosed in a small space. In Chicago, after the White Sox won the World Series, a bunch of us went to the celebratory parade. It was so crowded I couldn't move or see over the top of anyone's head. I had to find a less congested alley in order to catch my breath. "Yes," I replied, deciding this was a safe answer. "Yes, I am claustrophobic." The woman stared at my face, then sighed loudly and unapologetically as she lowered her eyelids to write something on her clipboard. She wore a small holiday pin near her name tag. The pin was a fuzzy snowman made of the palest blue felt. His arms stuck out from his sides in a T and were made of real twigs. Did she have a small child who glued it together for her? I pictured the child in school today, knowing his mom was wearing the pin he made, and I saw them talking about their days together over dinner, smiling and eating a favorite spaghetti recipe.

The woman finished her questions and appeared satisfied with her clipboard. She looked up and asked me if I had any questions.

I considered not going through with the MRI. It's my baby, my pregnancy, so everything is optional they tell me . . . right? The doctors were vague regarding what would happen next anyway, so in trying to do the right thing, I was confused as to why this kind of test was necessary and what we would find out. Was the test going to tell the doctors that everything would be OK? Would it assure me that I would be a good mother to a healthy baby boy or girl?

"Is the machine open? I mean, is it small?" I asked the woman with the pin.

"We don't use open MRI machines, but it's very big. You will be great."

I stepped into the vast white room and over to the MRI machine. The also white machine sat alone in the center of the room like an island, far away from the walls or any other equipment. I smiled at the staff sitting at their computers behind a rectangular pane of glass. A young male technician guided me onto the table and handed me a pair of headphones. I laid down, put the headphones on, and closed my eyes. David handed me my eye mask filled with lavender stones, and I asked him to place it over my eyes. The heavy mask filled my forehead and the area behind my eyes with a familiar darkness.

My body rolled into the machine, and I tried to pretend I wasn't there, that this wasn't happening, and I didn't even need this test. I tried to remain behind the spaces of my eyes and beneath the weight of the eye mask until the technician told me the test was done and I could come out.

Fully inside the machine, I imagined that my stomach looked like a giant beach ball under the hospital gown. It must have nearly touched the ceiling of the tube I was inside. I thought of Augustus in *Willy Wonka* when he got stuck in the vacuum cylinder. I smiled. When I did, the baby kicked. The baby kicked again, and I felt him or her rolling and stretching inside, like bubbles, shooting stars, and waterfalls.

A voice inside my headphones, someone from behind the pane of glass, told me not to move, not a single inch.

"Can you stay even more still? Just long enough to get some photos. We need the baby not to move either."

Was he serious? I couldn't control the baby moving inside me any more than I could control my anxiety inside this machine. With all my yoga knowledge and practice, I tried to imagine myself in savasana, the final resting pose at the end of class. But this machine was not my mat, and I couldn't pretend. I was on my back, but instead of the edges of my mat and the soft wooden floor, I felt hard plastic on my legs and back. I rubbed my toes together inside the now sweaty medical socks. My exposed shinbones turned cold while some sort of air blew directly on them.

Curious inside the machine, I fluttered my eyelids open to see where I was; it couldn't be that bad. I immediately shut them again, but it was too late. I did not like what I saw. And I was most definitely claustrophobic. As my breaths quickened, I stopped trying. I grabbed on to the slippery, curved sides of the machine. My body began to unravel and then collapse.

Using my elbows as leverage and scooting on my butt, I backed my oversized body out of the machine. As I wriggled and slid, the cotton gown stuck to my skin and to the hard plastic beneath me. I did not glide but squeaked all the way until my head was finally exposed to the room, next my shoulders, finally my stomach and legs.

"Can you stay still? Just a little longer."

The technicians frantically spoke to me from behind the glass wall. Their voices sounded robotic and automated through the intercom system and the ill-fitting headphones. I ignored their routine pleas and followed my body's signal to get out. I'm not sure if I was giving up or accepting my fate, but I could not ride this wave. I had no idea whether or not the actual test got to me or the entire crush of the experience itself.

I arrived outside the tube with sweat dripping from my neck and chest. My skin was lit on fire, and I tore off the hospital gown in front of everyone, uncaring about my exposed breasts, still panting while holding my belly. The crooked headphones tipped and fell off, and I hung my head in surrender. "I'm just going to have the baby."

I said these words first so I could hear them myself. Then I looked at the young male technician who stood next to me. "I'm just going to have the baby."

He didn't respond right away but held his gaze with mine.

"That's good," he said when he spoke, still keeping eye contact. "You did fine ... you did good, actually ... don't worry."

The young man's understanding and grace struck me, and I felt his permission to let go.

Something tense and pulling loosened. I unwound everything I had been holding together, and the undoing didn't kill me. In fact, I felt relief.

Once upstairs in the pediatric neurosurgeon's office, I explained that I couldn't go through with the MRI. In place of a name tag on his shirt, an engraved plaque sat on his desk next to framed photos of his children and wife. I noticed he had a dog, and they had all been kayaking on a small, frothing river.

"I had to go in one of those things once," Dr. Adler said reminiscently, as if preparing me for an adventure tale. "I couldn't believe how difficult it was. The only reason I stayed is because I make so many kids do it for me, and I can't believe how brave they are. I just played eighteen holes of golf in my head."

His reaction was more of a shrug. I assumed he would be mad, like I had wasted his time.

Dr. Adler sat behind his large desk but leaned toward me and my husband as if we were sitting around a table in a restaurant. I realized his concern was not with the test results or lack thereof. His concern was my intention. He matter-of-factly described how the brain works and its extreme tenderness during development. Dr. Adler had seen babies born without brains who barely stayed alive for a few minutes. He'd seen devastating brain disorders become known after birth that affected children for the rest of their lives. Brains are impossible to predict; babies and humans are impossible to safeguard. Through our conversation, I got the sense that our situation might not be dire, at least not yet, not until Dr. Adler could actually meet and examine the baby.

"If you've decided to have the baby, there is nothing else to do. BUT, until then, don't Google anything. Call me if you need something."

Dr. Adler led us out of his office and pointed to the elevator that would take us down.

We walked out of the twenty-story building a little lighter. After two weeks of waiting and expecting a scientific diagnosis that would either be devastating or uplifting, the best thing ever had happened. We still didn't have an answer about our baby; we had no MRI photos and no evidence. We had the same information we came with. Yet we were shown the power of neutrality in the moment, and that changed everything.

When I unwind my body from eagle pose, my limbs tingle with relief. The energy that has been pent up and twisted has space to relax and expand. And it expands further than it was able to before getting into the twist. I stand on one leg and then the other, ticking back and forth on my feet, now able to enjoy the freedom of the mat and the floor. I shake my arms out at my sides, and blood rushes down the back of my neck and spine. A silver glowing light reaches up my back, surrounds my shoulder blades, and explodes out the top of my head. Lightness envelops my body and my limbs, and I know the pose has expelled some necessary knots.

EIGHT

Tapas : Self-Discipline

"The Universe needs more Mothers,
regardless of birth or babies."

—Rebecca Campbell

The third niyama is tapas and means "self-discipline." The practice
of self-discipline gives us a choice: We can seek growth and opportunity, particularly when times are challenging or not what we imagined, or we can slip deeper into unawareness and angst. The word
tapas is derived from the root tap in Sanskrit, which means "to burn."
Tapas also refers to the burning that must take place for nature to
flourish and transform. Periodically, a controlled burn allows forests
or drylands to clear out excess, harmful growth. So too is the process
for us. Tapas teaches us that when we stay in the fire, despite discomfort, new possibilities about who we are and what we can accomplish
are made available to us. Are we willing to stay in order to see what's
on the other side? Do we possess the willingness and self-discipline
to endure change and let it scorch us so we may grow into something
new? Through the lens of tapas, self-discipline, motherhood—and
any life-changing event—becomes an opportunity to learn from our
daily practice.

BADDHA KONASANA

MOTHERHOOD GIVES US THE SAME OPPORTUNITY TO BECOME A
witness as yoga. Instead of grabbing at the next pose, the next
milestone, the next month with the baby, we can honor the practice
and the daily discipline. In yoga, coming to our mat is called sadhana,
which translates to "daily practice" or "spiritual practice." Like yoga,
motherhood contributes to our spiritual growth without us even realizing
it. By showing up everyday, motherhood teaches us forgiveness, staying
power, and compassion. Through the daily practice of motherhood, our

fears are illuminated, our illusions smashed, and our hearts are broken wide open.

As a new mom, I was determined to get everything right the first time. My lofty, idealistic expectations forced open a wound that had already taken root and exposed my insecurity, perfectionism, and my inner critic.

New motherhood did not match what I saw in magazines or in my mind, and the broken promise shocked me. I cried, I panicked, and I wondered how I would get through the fussy, sweaty, sleepless nights. Of course, my emotions felt highly selfish and invalid. Babies are supposed to make you happy, right?

When our emotions and our experience don't align with society's message, rather than question the message, we question ourselves. We disown the inner turmoil as well as our bodies. We vow to fit back into non-maternity jeans as soon as possible. We take care of the baby while we attempt to return to our old life. We fear that becoming a mother will take parts of us away, so we try to do it all, and we do it with a smile.

But like yoga, motherhood is not achieved through appearance; motherhood is achieved through practice. The reason yoga is called a practice is because we don't come into the room knowing every single pose or even one pose fully. In fact, even after years of continued practice, the amount to learn from a single pose is always different and the possibilities infinite. Asanas are not a finish line; they are an opportunity to discover something about yourself in the moment that is happening right now, where you are today. If we expect perfection—in motherhood or in yoga—if we do not accept the ups and downs, then we set ourselves up for failure, and we miss the valuable lessons that are taught to us through the difficult times as well as the joys. We miss the opportunity in every painful, hard, gut-wrenching, exhausted, messy, ugly, desperate part of the practice.

I sit down on my mat at the beginning of every yoga class, instinctively press the bottoms of my feet together, and let my knees fall out wide. In gym class as a kid, we called this "butterfly," and we would flap our knees up and down, up and down like wings while we held onto the toes of our gym shoes with our hands. I don't remember anything else from gym class growing up, just butterfly pose during every closing stretch. It's possible we were flapping away sadness, anger, fear, or any pent-up energy, and maybe that's why the exercise stays with me.

In yoga, the pose is called bound angle—baddha konasana in Sanskrit. After rolling my yoga mat onto the hardwood floor, I press and smooth the curled up edges and sit down firmly, grounding my pelvic bones to the earth like sunken anchors. I pull my legs up and in, and allow the soles of my feet to touch. I press the soft skin together like the pages of a book and hold my feet closed by wrapping my hands around my toes. As I do this, I tuck in my lower abdomen and make sure my back is straight and not arched. My knees fall out to the sides and nearly touch the floor without much effort. As I breathe, I inch my heels in closer to my groin and lean as far forward as I can without losing the straightness in my spine. With each half inch forward, ligaments deep inside my inner thighs stretch long, and my back gains length. Inhaling, I am here, present in this class. Exhaling, I let go of everything that came before this.

My father-in-law leaned over the back of the couch and peered lovingly at baby Bennett, finally asleep, swaddled tightly inside his Moses basket. From my spot on the other side of the couch, I noticed joy illuminate my father-in-law's face as he watched his new grandson sleep. He had just come from the office and wore a simple cotton t-shirt tucked into his black dress pants. It was a hot June day, and through our open windows I could hear people walking dogs and pushing children in strollers on the sidewalk below. I glanced down at my socks and pajamas and thought about what I would normally be doing on a sunny summer evening. Suddenly exhausted, I was ready to sleep myself.

"It's fun being a new mommy, isn't it?" My father-in-law said.

"Yeah." Even though it wasn't a question, I smiled and nodded back.

My heart opening as a result of new motherhood shook me the most. It wasn't the constant crying or the sore breasts or the change in sleep routine. The existing with my heart wide open is what rocked me, broke me, and made me want to put myself back together just as I was before having a baby. I grasped at things that would make me feel like my old, cocooned self. I wanted to fit back into my pre-pregnancy clothes. I wanted to go out to a restaurant and drink a glass of wine. I wanted to go back to work, shop with friends, watch a TV show with my husband on the couch without worrying if the baby would wake up. I wanted to be a good mother, but I'd never been a mother before, and the newness of my life lifted all my inadequacies to the surface like an undertow. I didn't like this. I didn't like being new at something. I wanted to be perfect from the start.

Intuitively, I breastfed the new baby in a version of bound angle pose, feet pressed together, knees wide and open. I moved one knee all the way down to the couch and used the other leg to help prop up my arm as I nursed the baby. Even though my position was lopsided, it was comfortable to let the baby nurse on that side as I leaned back onto pillows and breathed—inhale, exhale. Other than moving to the other breast, the other side, the baby and I sat like this all day. When he slept, I very carefully tucked him into the pale yellow basket my friend had given me, and I retreated to the kitchen to grab a snack. Or I lay on the long edge of the couch next to the baby and slept myself. As I practiced a little differently each day, motherhood and breastfeeding flowed or it didn't. I felt tired or I didn't. Confident as a mother, or completely failing. There seemed to be no in-between. I looked at my new son in the Moses basket. A friend had given it to me after using it with all three of her boys who were now school-age. Hand woven with pale yellow reeds and lined with soft, ivory fabric, the basket was quite an adorable place for a baby. It had two handles on the sides, each decorated with a tiny silk bow. For all purposes, it functioned as an actual basket. But, I was cautioned, it was not a good idea to actually carry the baby inside the basket as the handles were purely for decoration. Despite this impractical aspect, the basket did come in handy while sitting on the couch and created the perfect, magazine-worthy napping space for a baby.

"Well, I'm off but I'll stop by again tomorrow! I love you." My father-in-law kissed me on the forehead and gathered his things. As he clunked down the stairs and shut the door too loudly, Bennett jumped. His eyelids twitched briefly open and his arms came loose from the swaddle. I held my breath—please don't wake up, not yet. The baby wrinkled his nose, and his lips curled into a scowl, parting slightly as if he would scream. But then he settled back into his slumber, and I finally exhaled.

Me, the basket, and the baby had been on this couch for days. The practice felt the same each day—daunting, exhausting, and unsure. The basket and the baby were so delicate and tender. When Bennett slept in it, everything looked like a magical scene out of Pottery Barn's Nursery edition. And then there was me—unshowered, undressed, and unqualified.

Tears flooded my eyes and a knot formed in my stomach. How could I have been so naive? New babies are hard work. I was so in love, yet terrified at the same time. There were expectations around motherhood—elation, tenderness, beauty, and fulfillment.

Everyone else around me was overjoyed.

Is it OK to admit I was scared of my own baby?

ARDHA CHANDRASANA

Mastering ardha chandrasana (half moon pose) one day in class does not guarantee I will balance in it steadily the next. Some days I have unnerving focus in the one-legged, sideways balance pose. I don't even need my hand on the ground for support. My standing foot presses down onto the mat while my thigh muscles reach up. My torso bends sideways, and my other leg stretches straight out and perpendicular to the mat. I extend both arms in opposite directions, one hand toward the floor and the other to the sky. I am tipped over like a five-pointed star—here, present, and completely supported by my core.

The next day in class I completely fall out of ardha chandrasana, barely able to hold my leg up with my obliques. I cannot lift my supporting hand off the floor, and I need to use a block under my palm for raised assistance. It's hard to believe I am the same person today that I was yesterday. My fingers ache from the weight of my body, and my knuckles turn white from pressing so firmly against the block. Despite the soft pain and my inner frustration, I stay and I try, and I hope to regain my balance next time.

Instead of biting my teeth and gripping my toes on the mat in order to not fall out of half moon pose, I decide to trust my core and my limbs. I flex my foot and notice that my heel can still support me while stretching into the air. If I imagine well enough, I can feel a hard surface beneath the sole of my raised foot, as if I am pressing into a wall. Despite standing on one leg, both feet feel rooted firmly to the ground. I feel strong, supported by myself and by the earth.

The practice of tapas requires a gentle willingness to stay, not to prove something or look a certain way, but to maintain the desire and curiosity to be shown something new. Tapas reminds us that nothing is mastered. The practice of self-discipline is never-ending. One lesson will lead us directly to the next, but our endurance will be better as a result of our previous practice. To be transformed, we must return to our mat, to the slow burn, to our sadhana.

I trusted my body more when I let go of judgment. When I abandoned my image of what motherhood was supposed to look like—like the old version of me but with a baby—I could actually accept the way things were as a brand-new mom— unsure and struggling, ecstatic and in wonderment. I couldn't hide the fact that I was breastfeeding or that I had just given birth a few weeks ago. I couldn't hide the baby on a Friday night in the kitchen with our friends. I couldn't cover my exhaustion with makeup and long earrings because the covering up felt like manipulation and untruth, like everyone could see right through me.

I was surprised at how often people asked me, "Is he a good baby?"

Of course he is good, I thought. What else would a baby be? Were they asking if he sleeps? If he is quiet for long stretches of time? Or were they asking about me, am I OK? Am I a good mom? And is being a good mom somehow reflected in the baby?

Motherhood is not the image that had been fed to me by magazines or even doctors. Motherhood is soul work because it reveals the truth about preciousness, life, and love. New babies and the swelling of a heart do not necessarily feel hopeful or twinkling all the time. Sometimes new motherhood is dark, like rocking the baby in the nursery at 3 a.m. and feeling as if no one else exists or understands. Or like functioning on two hours of sleep but smiling anyway because you don't want to appear ungrateful. New motherhood is awakening in awe at how far women have been duped and marveling at the absurdity of the contradiction: the pulsing canyon that forms in your heart because you are so in love with your baby you don't want to miss a second, yet you are so exhausted you also want the whole thing to be over.

WHEN I GROW UP

When in kindergarten I was asked to announce to an entire auditorium full of people what I would be when I grew up. Huddled in the dimly lit stairway, I stood clumsily in line with the other kindergartners. A blue-and-white papier mâché helmet bobbling in front of me threatened to knock me over. We all had on awkwardly made outfits, costumes that symbolized our declared future profession.

The boy standing ahead of me wore an all gray sweatsuit. Blue construction-paper letters, sprinkled in silver glitter, spelled out NASA on the back of his shirt, and his large, handmade helmet still smelled of acrylic paint and drying glue. I looked down at the baby doll in my arms and adjusted her printed blanket so it wrapped tightly around her entire body, not hanging off, just like my mother showed me.

Little voices began to echo throughout the auditorium as each child took their turn on stage.

"When I grow up, I want to be a ballerina."

"When I grow up, I want to be a doctor."

"When I grow up, I want to be an astronaut."

When it was my turn, I walked slowly across the long stage and felt the heat from the overhead lights on my hair and face. I lowered my eyelids and tried to see the audience in front of me. My skirt hung too long and dragged on the slippery floor, so I took my steps very close together, careful not to trip on the beige polyester fabric. My mom found the skirt in the bottom drawer in her room where my sister and I were allowed to play dress-up. Since it was too big, my mom had rolled and pinned the waistband, which I clutched with my left hand while cradling the baby in my right arm. I got to center stage and adults' heads appeared as dark silhouettes under dusty beams of light. I didn't know where my own parents were. My throat swelled as my gaze remained, and I looked out. I lifted my chin until my lips reached the microphone and carefully, as practiced, recited my line: "When I grow up, I want to be a mommy."

The entire audience laughed.

I felt a sting at the center of my breastbone, and the lump in my throat expanded until I held my breath.

I stood still for another moment, and then, holding my baby doll tightly, I walked quickly offstage to protect her from their teasing.

My classmates behind me continued,
"When I grow up, I want to be a teacher."
"When I grow up, I want to be a veterinarian."
"When I grow up, I want to be a firefighter."

My son Andrew came home from kindergarten and handed me a yellow sheet of paper from his folder. I stood at the counter and began to read, and the familiar memory washed over me. Andrew's kindergarten class was working on a project—When I Grow Up—and it was to be performed during the spring concert.

I made note of the date and time and clipped the yellow sheet of paper to the refrigerator with a magnet. I stared for a while at the title—When I Grow Up. I glanced at the pot on the stove and the box of pasta waiting to be dropped into the water when it boiled. I shuffled to the cabinet in my socks and sweatpants and lifted four plates from the shelf.

"Boys!" I yelled, "Dinner will be ready soon!"

The following week, I couldn't find a parking spot in the already full lot at school, so I drove back out to the road and pulled behind another person's car who was also apparently late. I rushed briskly across the parking lot, and a mother I recognized from the school pick-up line whispered to me encouragingly, "You made it!" She handed me a program printed on green office paper, and I entered the auditorium. From the side of the room, I saw David sitting on a folding chair in the center row. He was bent over his phone but looked up in time to see me and gestured me over to the seat he had saved next to his.

I walked through the loud chatter of excited voices and inched sideways in front of the knees of already seated parents. I murmured "hi!" and "hello!" to each one and eventually made it to my husband.

"Hey," I said. "I couldn't find a spot."

"Yeah," he answered, still busy with his phone. "I figured."

I sat down and glanced around at the audience. Parents had their iphones and video cameras ready to go to document their child's turn on stage. I reached into my coat pocket for my own phone, pulled it out, and double checked that the ringer was pushed to silent. I glided the phone back into my pocket and checked to see Andrew's place in line. Seeing me, Andrew waved wildly from the side of the gym, and I waved excitedly back with the green paper program still in my hand. David's phone dinged loudly another time, and I glanced over just as the screen lit up. He hurriedly turned it off and shoved the phone into his own pocket, not even bothering to read the message. Right then, the lights dimmed and the music teacher ushered a line of thirty kindergartners onto the stage.

I inhaled and held my breath, my son's moment collapsing into mine, and my nerves from my own time on stage leaked open in anticipation of his performance. I searched the now full stage and spotted Andrew in the front row, behind a little girl wearing a sparkly tiara and a long, iridescent gown. David took his phone back out of his pocket and lifted it up over the heads of parents in front of us, ready to take a photo. I watched the screen intently from my chair as he zoomed in on Andrew and got him in perfect view.

A blonde-haired, blue-eyed girl gently touched her tiara before folding her hands together in front of her. Posed at the microphone, she recited her line: "When I grow up, I want to be a princess." The audience erupted in laughter.

I felt the sting of her promise, and my throat swelled from the familiar story. I am sure the little girl wondered what was wrong with her declaration? Is wanting to be a princess too silly or fantastical?

I wondered how many of us actually grow up and become what we said we would. I thought of the boy who stood in front of me with the blue-and-white papier mâché helmet and wondered if he was now an astronaut. I was a mother, just like I said I would be. And it did feel kind of cute and silly sometimes, just as the audience thought on that day. I wondered if becoming a mother twenty-six years later was my way of keeping a promise to myself and to everyone else, especially after declaring it on stage.

David straightened his arms to position his phone further out in front, ready for our son's turn. Andrew stepped up to his place on stage in his black hat and matching trench coat. I had wrapped the long black belt twice around his small waist and the tie hung stiffly near his right hip. Andrew paused, then proudly shouted into the microphone, "When I grow up, I want to be a detective!" The audience clapped and giggled, and Andrew grinned; he knew they approved.

As Andrew walked to the end of the line, David placed his phone face down on his lap, and we watched the rest of the kindergartners take their turns on stage. I made eye contact with Andrew who now stood along the side of the gym, and I gave him my proud thumbs-up. When all the students finished, the teachers wrangled the kindergartners out of the room, and parents stood up to leave.

David's phone dinged loudly from his lap, and my whole body jerked awake from my trance. I looked over and saw him putting on his coat. "Guess I'll see you at home." He smiled. "OK." I touched his arm, and he gave me a kiss on my cheek.

I listened to a guided meditation once by Deepak Chopra in which he talked about sequoia trees. He explained that they drop new seeds inside thick shells, and nothing can break them open. Nothing except fire. If it weren't for natural wildfires, the hard shells would never crack, and the seeds would never be spread in order to grow. The meditation reminded me of tapas, and the necessary burn I needed for my own heart to emerge. Tapas gives us a choice: stay in the fire to be transformed or turn away and head back toward the darkness, the illusion, and the comfortable indifference. We can show up to our practice ready to stay in the heat so we may break open to experience what is real, or we can miss the opportunity in the necessary albeit uncomfortable fire and stay the same.

Back in my car, I pull my phone out of my pocket and turn the ringer back on. I buckle my seatbelt and check the rearview mirror for cars pulling out behind me. All the cars are leaving at once. I pick up my phone again and look at Facebook as I wait my turn. I put my phone back in the car console and check my rearview mirror again to see if I can move.

Finally, I angle my car out into the line of traffic and begin to drive. My mind wanders back to the performance, the auditorium, David's phone dinging, and his screen . . . David was texting someone during the performance. All of a sudden, while signaling to turn out of the school parking lot and onto the main road, a woman's name floats to the surface of my mind, as if emerging from beneath a murky sea. The person David was texting was named Nicole Weston. I see her name clearly, bobbing on the surface of a calm wave. But we don't know anyone named Nicole. The woman's name submerges into darkness as quickly as it appears. I click on my right turn signal and speed up the car toward home.

Her name is so fleeting, I don't think about it for months after this vision. The pertinent information sinks away beneath the tide, ready to re-emerge only when I am ready to see it.

NINE

Svadhyaya : Self-Study

"When physical and mental purification begins
to take place through yoga sadhana, it's at
the same time you begin to see both your
faults and good qualities very clearly."

—Swami Kripalu

The fourth niyama is svadhyaya and means "self-study." We practice
yoga to clearly witness ourselves—a process of unwrapping roles,
identities, and facades—in order to arrive at the core. When we are
able to see ourself clearly, we bring awareness to things we want to
change. Observing faults is a powerful spiritual practice, and brings
out beautiful qualities like acceptance, humility, and an unshakeable
strength. Svadhyaya teaches us how to compassionately address and
peel away layers of false self in order to see the truth underneath: the
diamond, the indestructible center.

ADDICTED

MY EYES STILL HEAVILY CLOSED, I AM NOT READY TO WAKE UP. IT IS
Sunday, and I want to sleep in. My neck aches from the pillow,
and my damp, sweaty hair sticks to the stiff, cotton fabric. I can tell it
is morning because I sense sunlight beating down on top of my closed
eyelids. I can hear Bennett and Andrew laughing and playing. They are
talking to David about making pancakes and to be sure to add vanilla.
For a moment I am disoriented because I assume I am in my bed, yet the
boys and their laughter sound so close. A tucked away memory emerges.
I am brought back to the gym where I took yoga many years ago; the
children's laughter I heard that day in savasana was just like what is
happening now with my own children. Was the dream a premonition?
Did my soul know I would be here?

The eerie, deja-vu experience forces my eyelids open, and I realize I am on the couch in the living room. I probably fell asleep here last night, and David decided to leave me instead of carrying me upstairs to our bed. A cushion is wedged behind my head as a pillow and a blanket from the couch covers my body. My head throbs from drinking too much wine last night. Seeing my movement, the boys now circle around me in a flurry of footsteps and laughter.

"Mommy! We're making pancakes! Mommy! You're awake!"

Their energy makes me feel overwhelmed and ashamed all at once. I vow I will not drink tonight—just for one night.

The first glass of wine I had after nine months of pregnancy and giving birth was a large, round glass of deep red on Father's Day. With the half-empty glass on the table in front of me, purple residue staining the insides, a calm blanket washed over me, and the anxiety of new motherhood flowed right through my limbs and out the top of my head. I smiled. I smiled at my husband and my father-in-law. I smiled at the baby. My sore breasts disappeared, and I no longer cared about my still protruding stomach. Numbed, the tired circles under my eyes made no difference to me anymore.

After bringing the baby home, I felt a disconnect between my image of motherhood and my reality. The nursery looked sweet and soft, but the baby cried shrilly. We cuddled and stared into each other's eyes, but I often had to ask myself: *Am I worthy of nurturing such a beautiful creature?* Half a glass of wine was just enough to take the edge off, to blur my senses and alleviate all the fears I had about being an inadequate mother. I could look my husband in the eyes and listen to him discuss his work day. I could carry on a conversation with my father-in-law without checking on the baby every five seconds. I could relax and join in with society.

I get off the couch and help the boys and David finish the pancakes. I pile several of the light, fluffy circles onto a plate for myself and let the boys slather them with butter and syrup. I eagerly sit down to eat and enjoy each delicious bite as the boys tell me exactly what they did to help. Andrew cracked an egg and Bennett added the vanilla, which is their secret ingredient.

David returned late last night from a business trip. I was already on the couch on my third glass of wine when he walked in. After cleaning up the breakfast dishes, I fold the blanket over the back of the couch and go to check the recycling bin. The empty bottle of wine is there. Lately, I have been retracing my steps in order to put my evenings together. My mind fogs up easily, especially after wine, and I need to check what and how much I drink. My damp toothbrush tells me I had brushed my teeth. The wet hand towel in the bathroom signifies I had washed my face. The shiny dishes next to the sink tell me I made dinner and cleaned up after. Lately, I remember pouring the first glass and then nothing after that.

After breakfast David goes upstairs to unpack. I put a show on the TV for the boys and hear the shower turn on. David's backpack sits unzipped on the hallway floor. The fire on the back of my neck intensifies as I reach my hand inside the front pocket. I hear the shower running and listen acutely for the water to turn off.

I thumb through his day planner and find organized receipts inside the front pocket that all make sense for a work trip. Ashamed and a little deflated, I put everything back and hear the shower turn off. I pull myself up the stairs to change for yoga.

I twist my unwashed hair into a bun, slam the car door, and walk briskly to the small house that serves as a yoga studio. The coffee shop/ yoga studio/greenhouse sits on the corner of a busy intersection at one of the few stoplights in town. A well-lit hospital runs continuously on the opposite side of the street, and I often see nurses make their way down the grassy hill and across the median in their scrubs, bringing coffee back to their worn-out colleagues. The barren patio of the unique coffee shop turns into a lush greenhouse during spring and summer. Ferns dangle over the edges of stone pavers and colorful flower trays overflow onto tables, an invitation for customers to wander outside with their cup. The yoga house floats calmly in the center, set back from the busy road between the coffee shop and a large barn used for weddings and events.

I close the glass door of the studio behind me, which immediately silences nearby sounds of traffic. I yank on my bun one last time to loosen a few strands and unwedge my yoga mat from under my arm. The fireplace is on, even though it is mid-April. Spring has been undecided about her arrival to Wisconsin.

The parking lot is full of weekend customers, and I scan the wooden floor for an open spot for my mat. Yesterday morning it was only me and one other student, so we spread out into an open triangle with the teacher and leisurely went through our practice. Today the room chatters with everyone's weekend plans and social obligations. Yoga is an in-between, a calm before a storm, an exhale before the fervor. I step out of my flip flops and kick them into the disheveled collection near the door. I roll out my mat right in front of the shoe pile, and sit down inside a warm beam of sunshine.

To begin, the instructor asks us to set our intention for the day, like forgiveness, patience, or strength. She clarifies that our intention could be for ourself or someone else, and we should welcome the feeling into our consciousness and our practice.

While contemplating my intention, I sit in cross-legged pose with my eyes closed. My hands rest heavily on my knees, and my palms face up to the sky. I found nothing in David's backpack during my digging and am desperate to know whether or not he is cheating, so I ask the universe for a sign. Despite the open palms in my lap, I offer my intention with clenched fists. I don't ask; I plead. My request is insistent rather than vulnerable, more of a demand than an intention: *God, I don't want to twist my body during yoga anymore and wait for clarity. I'm too impatient and it's too hard to have faith. I don't want to search for elusive signs from my heart through mediation or journaling. I just want to be delivered the instructions and act accordingly. I believe in you, God, so won't you help me? Tell me what to do, and I'll do it.*

I'm not open or willing, so any sign received will be easily funneled through my human rationalization until it is my own will and not a sign at all. The answer will be a mess, and I will still be full of resistance and confusion. Until I let go, until I am willing to see clearly, I will continue to fight to get my way.

Even though I can't find evidence, my search has turned up some questions: Without proof, is my unease a good enough reason to end my marriage? Is the problem me and my drinking, or am I drinking because of him? And which came first? Am I really unhappy or just bored? Can I take back the promise I made ten years ago? And most importantly, what would people think?

Asking questions often leads to bigger, deeper, and more meaningful questions. My real fear is that I have no idea who I am if David doesn't love me. When I walked down the aisle on our wedding day, I handed over my entire identity to him. I was committed to making him happy, at any cost. Who am I if not his wife? And who else would want me?

I twist, lean, and hold my body through poses during class until we finally lay down for savasana. I try to relax. My head swirls, still dizzy from the night before. When David got home from his trip, he sat and watched the end of the movie with me. His phone fell out of his pocket and onto the couch. He picked it up from the cushion, stood up, and shoved it into his back pocket before walking to the bathroom. I stayed tucked inside my warm blanket, safely numbed from my bottle of wine.

I realize I only see his phone in his back pocket lately. He used to leave it out on the couch or on the counter. But not lately and not for months. We also haven't had sex in over seven months. I asked him why one day, and he told me he didn't feel close to me that way. My interpretation of his words was that I must be ugly, my body ruined from childbirth and age.

All these thoughts surface in savasana, forcing my muscles to grip and twitch while lying on my mat. My skin grabs at the soft rubber as if hanging on to my last minutes of peace. I inhale deeply, tense all my muscles, and let my limbs go limp and numb at my sides. With class almost over, I have to concentrate that much harder to stay. The floorboards creak and groan under my restless body. The sunbeam that warmed my mat at the beginning of class has clouded over and leaves a dull, gray chill. I want to run away, ignore, and squish out my feelings of love and loss, but the truth is under my skin, inside my throat, and audible in the grumbling floorboards beneath me.

The truth is I do love him, I still love him, and it hurts that he no longer loves me back. Whether there is another woman or not, I hurt a lot.

In order to practice svadhyaya, we need to be willing to look at our discomfort and turmoil and inquire into its source. I am fearful that David is having an affair, but all this projection onto him and his actions prevents me from looking at myself and my addiction. I don't want to see our unhappiness. I don't want to get divorced. I don't want to be wrong about the man I chose to marry or about marriage in general. I am wrapped up in the roles society has placed on me, in the belief system my family instilled in me, and in the fear of letting everyone down. I am working so hard at hanging onto my role, I have forgotten every single part of who I am.

In savasana, the pose during which we are meant to bear witness, my urge to cling and control heightens. I think of hiding places in the house where I have not looked. I hatch a plan for getting into David's phone. My friend Sam told me her strategy to confirm if her husband was having an affair. She texted me one night while they were at her in-law's lakehouse.

"I got Tom's password."

"What? How did you get it?"

"I watched him enter it and then repeated the numbers over and over in my head until I had time to write them down."

David always leaves his phone charging on the floor inside his closet. After hearing about Sam's strategy, I decide I will try the same. Maybe, once I get the password, I can wake up in the middle of the night and check his phone while he sleeps.

Just as I finalize my plan and give my body over to gravity and the floor, the faint ding of the instructor's cymbals alerts us it is time to come out. The high sound amid the silence startles me, and my body jerks awake, unready to leave my mat and return home.

TEN

Ishvara Pranidhana : Surrender

"Accepting pain as help for purification, study of
spiritual books and surrender to the Supreme
Being constitute yoga in practice."

—Sri Swami Satchidananda,
The Yoga Sutras of Patanjali, Book 2, Verse 1

The fifth niyama is ishvara pranidhana and means "surrender." To
surrender is to offer our actions as well as their results up to a higher
power—to our version of God, our higher self, or divine love. In yoga
and in life, it's important to know when to rest and when to trust.
We can make ourselves crazy thinking we have so much to do and
someone to be. In all the doing, it's important to remember that
we can also release our troubles up to something outside ourself.
Surrender is a continual practice. Just as we learn to let go of control,
we take it back, and need to let go again.

One way we attempt to hang on to an illusion of control is by trying to
prevent past pain from occurring again. We may not even know we are
doing this, but our body will instinctively remember an old trauma and
will necessarily be protective around a similar trigger. Feelings of being
unsafe or unsupported as a child or a sense of abandonment from a
past relationship will inevitably seep into a current one. Like augering
an archaeological site in order to remove unnecessary debris from an
artifact, a painful experience will remain in our body until it is addressed
and excavated. Self-study, the fourth niyama, tells us we can't be afraid
to dig in order to uncover what is true about ourselves. Are we acting out
of a past story, a past pain point, or are we actually seeing what is real?

Surrender, the fifth niyama, reminds us that we are never alone and
always supported by life and what the universe has in store for us.
Practicing both the fourth and fifth niyamas together gives us the

strength to move forward without fear of falling because we know that when a circumstance threatens to take us under, we have our practice of surrender. We can simultaneously engage in the action of examining our emotions in the current state as well as releasing the outcome. We can look while also letting go. Part of the practice of surrender is to become a nonjudgmental witness. Discovering and dusting off old pain stories, parts of ourselves we've buried due to grief and shame, takes first an increase in our awareness and a shift in our gaze.

UTKATA KONASANA

"LET'S MOVE INTO GODDESS, MY FAVORITE POSE!" SAYS ANDREA, MY instructor, the next day in class. She directs the students and we follow. My body is sideways, feet wide apart and pointed out in second position, and my thighs are nearly parallel to the ground like I am straddling a horse.

"Engage your inner thighs and activate your mulabhanda, your root chakra." (These stretches are known in the medical world as Kegels.)

I squeeze the muscles at my root chakra and sit my butt closer to the ground. I lengthen my upper body while simultaneously engaging my thighs in order to ground and stabilize my lower half. I extend my arms out and above my head for balance, like a dancer.

"Feel free to use lotus hands at your heart." Andrea shows us how to open our hands from prayer pose. I bend my elbows in as she demonstrates. Andrea is young, enthusiastic, and sexy. Her powerful description of our mulabhanda and red lotus fingers sends a tingle up my thighs. I keep my thumbs and pinkie fingers touching, as well as the bottoms of my palms. Then I open all my fingers into a lotus flower shape and picture them as crimson red petals. Energy surrounds me. I root to the mat while being light in my upper half. I squeeze my Kegel muscles tightly while trying not to also hold my breath.

Engagement of my root chakra adds strength and support in utkata konasana (goddess pose), a safe and steady base. Our root chakra is just this—a support, a part of our body that grounds us, not only physically but also emotionally. The root chakra is the foundation of all the chakras above it. So when our root is imbalanced, if our safety is in question, everything else becomes affected—our beliefs, our reactions, our perceptions, and our behaviors. We act out of fear rather than faith.

In utkata konasana, while enacting mulabhanda and using the lotus hands to enact faith, I can look because I am strong. I can look while feeling safe because I am supported by something outside myself.

I observe David and his phone intently for the next several days. After many trials, I finally watch him enter all four numbers of his password into his phone. I run for a Post-it note and jot down the code. My breath flutters and my low belly trembles; I feel closer to victory. A cool shiver wiggles down from my throat and into my navel. What is the truth? I feel high with anticipation. The need to know consumes me.

Another aspect of ishvara pranidhana is acceptance. When we can accept what is, we do not feel the need to take action or manipulate. Accepting that life is not the way we pictured, marriage is not what we expected, or our own sense of love is not the romantic fairytale we've been fed can bring us a sense of calm abiding. Much of our suffering derives from a belief that something is wrong, when in reality, it might just be life as it is right now. Not happy all the time. Not easy all the time. But necessary to uncover lessons and create growth, and all the while we are protected.

A RETURN TO BALASANA

When you leave during dark mornings, the sound of the garage door opening always wakes me. I feel you kiss my forehead, but I never open my eyes. I wait until the car pulls out of the driveway, accelerates down the road, and eventually, drives completely away. In the tender black silence, I wrap the covers closely around me and roll onto my right side. I inhale and exhale, and my heart thumps heavily inside my chest. I wait for the rapid beating to calm down, and I drift back to sleep. I'm enveloped in the in-between, the questioning in my mind, the doubting, the nagging loneliness I cannot place. All the enduring, during.

I have a nagging secret of my own. I'm not the same person you married. I thought being married was a safety net from having to compare myself to another woman, from words she delicately whispers into your ear, ways she moves her body under yours in bed, how her breasts feel fuller than mine in your hands.

My daily breaths are short and fast, agitated by our loveless life together. I never considered that taking care of children and a husband would drain me. I expected it to fulfill me, to complete and sustain me. But I've lost myself. In taking care of everyone else, I have not attended to my own breath, my own life force.

I follow the womanly path as demonstrated by my mother and grandmother. I follow along with people's expectations and assume their ambitions are also my own. I interpret being a woman as a collective undertaking, and if I just do as everyone else, happiness will find me. On the surface, I am good at being a wife and mother. But my breath is not full or expansive. The depth and range of being human do not interest me. I am shallow, and I only want to feel good all the time. The weight of an uncomfortable emotion presses on my chest and abdomen and feels like being buried in wet sand, so I hastily drag myself out by reaching for a drink or distraction. I am judgmental of myself and of others. I do not trust other people's happiness because I desperately crave what they have. Contentment, I believe, is owed to me, so I disallow feelings of grief and anger for fear that their opposing forces to happiness will sink me like quicksand, and I will never emerge. But my body wants to experience the full capacity of human emotion, so eventually, this type of ego-focused thinking is unsustainable. No matter how much good I collect, nothing fills the void of low self-worth and nonacceptance.

I know you might not love me anymore. I know there could be someone else, and the not knowing, but suspecting, wakes me up at night. My mind focuses keenly on the answer, rather than the question of how it all makes me feel and the question of what I want to do about it.

I slowly learn the benefit of surrendering to child's pose during a strenuous yoga series. I learn to hold on to my whole self, just as I am in that moment. I lend my body grace and spread my knees out to the edges of my mat, fold forward, and allow my belly to release heavily between my thighs. It is the only time my stomach does not feel the need to stay taught and sucked in. My post-children body is free to droop and expand between my legs with each full inhale without caring how other people see it, without caring how I see it. I let the smell of my exhale seep into my nostrils as I breathe deeply into the small triangular space created between my body and my mat. I feel my lower back sink, and I move my outstretched arms back and along my sides, palms facing up.

As my hands lay open, fists unclenched, I release my attachment to what my marriage or my body should look like. I loosen the tightness in my jaw by gently touching the tip of my tongue to the back of my top teeth, and then letting it fall into rest. My cradling arms envelop me like warm bed sheets, and I allow my entire body to be completely supported by the floor. I allow myself to breathe fully in balasana. In the day to day, I hardly ever surrender to my breath and what it tries to tell me.

Society conditions us to be ruthless in order to expect results, and to fixate on goals and pursue them at all costs, even at the expense of our own pain and suffering. In fact, sometimes we even believe pain and suffering are necessary to attain what we want. We're not used to letting go and allowing grace to step in; letting go feels weak and apathetic, like nothing will ever get done. But when you finally do surrender, when you give up control of your life and offer it up to your personal idea of God or the universe, grace does step in, and the outcome is better than you imagined.

Surrender is understandably the final principle of the niyamas and requires all nine that come before it. We cannot accomplish self-care, self-acceptance, self-love, or any of the yamas and niyamas without a bit of letting go.

David has just come back from another trip. I read in bed as he unpacks his toiletries, hangs his dress shirts in the closet, and plugs his phone into the charger on the floor. I continue reading until David switches off his light, and I wait for his breath to sound like steadily moving waves.

I slowly turn back the covers and crawl as quietly as possible out of bed. I turn to watch David for any movement. My feet pad tenderly across the soft carpet and I make my way to where his phone lay dark and asleep on the floor. I bend down and turn again, but David's breath continues to roll evenly with no sign of disturbance. I touch my finger to the black screen, and its immediate illumination startles me. I enter the four numbers I have now memorized, and the phone whirls itself awake like a genie emerging from a bottle.

I am in. First, I look at text messages. But they are empty. I check his email, but it is locked with a different password. Darn. I check his Facebook messages. He has just become friends with a man named Matt from Colorado, the same place he just traveled. I read the messages and learn that they went out for work drinks that turned into all-night drinks. Matt was unable to drive himself home so he stayed in David's hotel room. "Thanks for letting me crash, bud."

I know from David's history that his business trips can get wild. No one has families or spouses to worry about at the end of the day. No home to return to; no kids to kiss goodnight. They drown themselves in drinks to numb the pain of being away, the pain of the realization that this is their life, or the pain of not admitting what they really want in life. Then they finally pass out in whatever hotel, whatever city they are in, and shrug the whole experience off by the next day. "That was a crazy night! I don't need that again."

But then they do it all over again. The next trip, the next round of drinks, the only way to pass the time or hide from themselves.

I have no idea who Matt is or what happened on this night. My search has made me feel worse and not better. I couldn't find any evidence of an affair, only a drunken work trip, which was so normal it didn't cause me alarm.

I try again to get into David's email. I enter several password combinations that I think he might choose, but none of them work, and I don't want to lock him out of his account because then he would be suspicious.

I let go of my search for the moment. I decide it's not time for me to know. I set the phone on the floor and allow it to go dark again. I walk to the boys' rooms and touch each of their foreheads with my hand. I listen to their soft inhales through tiny nostrils. Then I return to my and David's bedroom, slip my body quietly back under the covers, and roll over to sleep.

KAPOTASANA : PIGEON POSE

PART III

Asana : Physical Practice

HEALING STARTS IN THE BODY

"Yoga is not a work-out, it is a work-in. And this is the
point of spiritual practice; to make us teachable; to open
up our hearts and focus our awareness so that we can
know what we already know and be who we already are."

—Rolf Gates

The third limb of yoga, asana, is our physical practice. We attend yoga class or follow a video. We do a home practice. We move our bodies through poses, and we expect something back, not only physically but emotionally, like insight, a calm mind, or a break from the outside world. We've all been taught about the body in terms of its physical appearance and abilities. No matter where we are, we are aware of our bodies: while shopping, watching a movie, or crossing the street. But many of us mistake our body for the enemy.

In yoga I treat myself more kindly. When I need a rest, I offer myself child's pose, puppy pose, or savasana. I ignore my usual tendency to master every pose and to "do my best." Yoga makes me question the obsession I have with my body, needing it to be beautiful yet hating it at the same time. Yoga teaches me to be more accepting.

Healing starts in the body, especially when we have remained separate from and have condemned our bodies for a long time. The daily practice of asana teaches us that our body exists, but not for others' pleasure or approval. Our body exists as an access point to our soul, the very part of us we need to listen to and depend on. Eckhart Tolle refers to our emotional body as the pain body and explains that anytime we are unaware or not present, we are allowing our past pain and trauma to run our current situation. When we shine awareness on the pain body, on the beliefs and experiences from our past, the pain body automatically loses power, and we can more easily act in accord with who we are.

ELEVEN

The Body

"The voice in the head tells a story that
the body believes in and reacts to."

—Eckhart Tolle

PAIN BODY

I WAS TEN THE FIRST TIME I HATED MY BODY. I WAS IN MY FRIEND TESSA'S bedroom and five girls including me were hanging out in our swim suits. It was summer and we had just walked up from the lake. At that age, we rarely wore more than a swimsuit in the summer in our small lake town, only flip flops or jelly shoes, no t-shirt or shorts. We roamed around in packs, bare-legged up to our hips, and innocently unaware that anyone would notice or care. We certainly didn't.

A sense of my body and how it should look came crashing into me on this day. And I have never recovered.

One friend pinched the skin above her bikini bottoms and commented, "Ugh, I'm sooooo fat!" She flopped her body across the bed and opened her older sister's *Cosmopolitan* magazine. The girl's comment was more like repeating a slogan than an actual observation that had come from her, a way to fit in and feel older than ten. This is how older girls stand, with their hands on their hips. And this is how older girls talk as they eye and pinch flesh from their bodies. And I wanted to be an older girl.

Her words slammed into me like a car that came out of nowhere as I merrily drove along. I swerved and looked down at my own stomach. For the first time I noticed how the skin rolled over itself where the edge of my suit met my body. Heat spread across the back of my neck as I realized this was not attractive. I should have curves going inward toward my hips, and the skin on my belly should be taught and defined, not wrinkled or bulging when I sat down. In a matter of seconds, my body that I had never really given much attention seemed full of flaws and ugliness. How could it be so obvious? Yet all this time I didn't know?

From that day, my body was no longer a part of me, and yet it consumed all of me. Even parts of my body that I liked were compared to the body parts on someone else, so there was always something to change, always something to mold and manipulate. What I didn't know is that when I determined my body to be something for others and an object for approval, I slyly gave myself the opportunity to never be enough and to always strive for more. At least on the surface, there was always room for improvement.

In yoga, I saw that my body was actually right; my body already knew what I needed to do, though my rational mind couldn't process it. Slowly and without realizing it, I began to see myself with compassion. I didn't hit my mat with a goal to sweat or strain. I came to class open and ready to receive. I paused and I breathed. I bent over and cried. I fell out of balance poses and then returned to them. I learned about my resilience. I learned about my capacity to trust. Even though the words had been said a million times before, for the first time, I actually heard them: *Be kind to yourself. Allow yourself rest. Allow yourself forgiveness. Trust your body.*

The compassionate words of yoga philosophy washed over me and penetrated my body's cells. Through continued practice, the loving wisdom took root a little more deeply. *Trust your body. Stay and listen, instead of pushing through.* In the midst of my practice, I slowly began the healing process of welcoming my body back into my life.

Shortly after having our first baby, David bought me a massage at my favorite healing spa in Chicago—the Ruby Room. On a Thursday evening, as dusk loomed, I made sure Bennett was changed, fed, and comfortable. David assured me they would both be fine. I opened the fridge to recheck the small bottle of yellowish breast milk sitting on the top shelf. I touched the plastic container lightly with my fingertips to affirm that I had left it there and that my leaving for the massage was not selfish.

I stepped out the front door and onto the sidewalk and made my habitual turn to the left on my way to the subway. Orange-purplish-hued clouds settled in around me, reminding me of the color of my favorite comforter from college. Walking outside the home and into the night, I felt alone—really alone, like something was missing. It was odd knowing my baby existed even though I couldn't see him. It was odd walking around outside, heels knocking on the pavement, without the baby attached to me in some fashion. Once on the El Train, I looked around at passengers reading books and holding small children, the crowds of people all crammed into the train to create a palette that represented the city. I stood inside a space between a woman's knees and a man's briefcase and held onto the metal hand rail, blending in.

I hadn't been out of the house in weeks. The baby and I had been in our own world, separate from everyone else in the city, hiding upstairs in the third-floor walk-up. And despite sitting on the train in my city as I always had, I no longer felt connected. In fact, a small panic spread over me as I thought about my new life with the baby and wondered if I'd ever feel like myself again.

By the time I walked upstairs and out of the underground subway, the sky had become completely dark. Streetlights glowed with hazy yellow brims, and the work crowd had transitioned into bar patrons. The scent of alcohol and the shouts of voices floated in and out of open doorways as I walked to my destination. I approached the spa and pulled open the heavy glass door that led me into a small foyer. Punchy citrus oil and sweet lavender hit my face and moved into my nostrils. I walked through a narrow doorway framed with a long red curtain on one side. The thick velvety fabric brushed my arm as I entered a larger, more brightly lit showroom. Water trickled down slabs of rock that hung on the walls and dripped playfully onto small rocks that sat in trays below. Handfuls of stones piled high like color-coordinated jelly beans sat in small bowls on a round table in the center of the room. Each bowl had a white label sticking out of it, indicating the name and healing properties of each stone. I checked in with the woman behind the desk. She wore a long, shimmery necklace with a pointed pink crystal dangling off the delicate chain— rose quartz was my guess. Her hair was cut short in a bright blonde pixie style that matched her defined cheekbones and swashes of magenta blush. After taking my name and checking my appointment in the computer, she led me to a waiting room near the back of the shop. The lights dimmed as we exited the main showroom and entered a hallway-like space. Plush, decorative pillows lined a long bench underneath a window that looked out onto the brick-walled alley. I sat and adjusted one of the red-and-purple striped pillows more comfortably behind my back. Not long after the pixie woman left, another woman entered the narrow sitting room from an adjacent door. I noticed her long, blue scarf, hanging perfectly from her shoulders and ending just below her waist. Ivory tassels waved gracefully along her thighs as she walked toward me.

"Molly?"

"Yes, hi!" I stood up and shook her extended hand.

"I know you're here for a massage, but I'm going to ask you to pick a card. It will help me to know where to focus my energy." As if beginning a magic trick, the woman fanned a deck of dark-reddish cards in front of me. The cards' edges were soft and worn, and thin white cracks meandered lovingly across the backs of their surface. I pulled a card from the spray, and as expected, it felt like used leather in my hand. I flipped it over and we both looked at the diagnosis—throat chakra. I had just gotten over another case of strep throat, a physical illness that had been chronic for my entire life. Not enough sleep, stress, or an unhealthy lifestyle brought it back to me every time, and antibiotics no longer got rid of it. Of course, the woman with the card deck didn't know any of this. She asked me what the card meant to me. We talked briefly about my strep throat issue and the new baby. After nodding in understanding, she led me into yet another room and pointed to a white robe folded neatly on the massage table. She exited the room to give me privacy, and I followed her instructions to undress and lie down on the warm, covered table. With a gentle rap on the door, the woman reentered and asked if she may read my aura. I had no idea what she meant, but I responded, "Yes! Go for it!" I closed my eyes and waited. Through the closed door, I could still hear the water dripping and falling from the showroom up front. After a few minutes of silence, the woman told me my aura was strong, meaning she could see it clearly. She said it was bright and light, and expanded enthusiastically throughout the room. She went on to explain that my aura even seeped into the hallway, under the doors, and into the rooms of other people receiving treatments at the spa. I imagined my aura also reaching out the front door, down the street, up the stairs of our apartment, and into the baby's nursery. "Let's try pulling this back in." The woman suggested that I keep more energy for myself. Too much was going outward, leaving nothing for me. I closed my eyes and opened myself to her visualization. I allowed a stream of light to make its way down Ashland Avenue, around the corner of Huron Street, and remain with the baby. But the rest of the energy, I took back. I started with the little rooms down the hall, and as I slowly pulled the light in around me, a bright white halo enveloped my entire body. As I did this, the warmth of the table below me became noticeably hotter. At first it felt warm and comforting, but as the heat intensified, I got nervous. The white halo around me started to feel constricting and heavy, as if being trapped in a small space, unable to stretch my arms or legs. My breaths became brief and shallow, and I was unable to take a complete inhale. The heat from the table moved off the back of my body and around to the front to my shoulders, my chest, and the tops of my thighs. "How are you?" Crystal asked. (This was not her real name, but what I began to call her.) She talked about crystals nonstop and their healing properties; she suggested I wander upstairs to the crystal showroom and try some, explaining that I wouldn't have to do anything—the right crystal would pick me. I told Crystal I would go upstairs after my appointment, but I knew it was a lie. I might have been tempted to believe this woman and the magic of the cards and the crystals, but in my head I heard the voices of my husband and my dad who told me I couldn't trust people; they were only trying to sell me something. My body was now physically shaking, almost convulsing, and I couldn't get it to stop. Embarrassed, I pulled in on my abs in an effort to keep my limbs still. I pressed my arms and legs down flat on the table, all the while still shaking and twitching. Sweat dripped into the crevice in the middle of my chest. My milk let down, and the pressure stung my breasts as they hardened and filled. "I hate it." I replied honestly to Crystal. "I am sweating and anxious. My stomach hurts. I can't stay still."

"OK, let it go."

"What?" I asked.

"Let it all out." Crystal said. "It's where you're comfortable. You don't need to keep your aura for yourself. Just let it all go, and let's see how you feel." With Crystal's permission, I released everything and probably more. I released my fear of being a new mom and my frustration with my body. I released the constriction of being the perfect wife, despite being an exhausted mother. I exhaled hugely and deeply, and allowed my limbs to fall out. I saw my aura spread wide and away from me. I saw my body relent to its nature and my light stream down the hall and underneath doorways where other women lay. My entire self filled the building, moved upstairs, down the city streets, up to the sky, and everywhere it could possibly reach. Calm washed over me. I felt so much better. With my aura extended and wandering, Crystal suggested we do something to bring attention and protection to my throat in order to care for it, in order for it not to be at everyone's mercy. Again, I listened to her voice and followed her prompts. She led me through an exercise during which I saw warm water rushing around my neck, wrapping down and around my throat and chest like a silky scarf. The scarf was made of water, and I could hear it moving, washing, keeping my neck warm and covered. The healing water especially pooled at the center of my throat and lapped tenderly at my skin. I left the massage with a sense that something profound had occurred. Walking back to the subway, I still had the waterfall scarf wrapped tightly around my neck, pulsing with shimmering blue energy at my throat center. I never did wander upstairs to the crystal showroom; despite my intense experience, I was still skeptical, and I needed to get home to the baby. Looking back, I wish I would have had the sense to get the woman's name and information. Today she remains like a ghost in my memory, a premonition of healing rather than an actual person. For that rare moment, I actually felt in control of my own body, not in my usual way of manipulating it to do what I wanted, but in a way that was accepting, humble, compassionate, and kind. My body didn't feel like nourishment for a growing baby or an object for some man's whim. My body felt like my own, a powerful form capable of moving energy and capable of taking care of me.

If I needed more reassurance that something other-worldly occurred during that appointment, my pesky strep throat has never returned in over twelve years since that day.

ROCK BOTTOM

On a chilly November morning, I waver tenuously into yoga class and sit down on my mat. I fold over into child's pose, let my forehead meet solid earth, and breathe through an open mouth. The shot of vodka I drank right before class in order to prevent the shakes permeates my exhale and lingers putridly above my mat. My sweaty hands stick to the rubbery surface, and I press the skin of my palms down deeper, as if trying to hang on. My fragile fingers still tremble with physical craving. Fire dances just above my skin as if someone had lit a match and set all the fine hairs ablaze. I smell the hot alcohol on my breath and the smoking hairs of my ignited, pleading flesh.

Could yoga class cure this deep yearning from my body and my soul? I want to be open, but instead all I can do is collapse.

There is one other woman in the class flowing easily through sun salutations as our instructor cues. I stay. The teacher's voice dulls into the background, and I remain bent over, huddled in child's pose, and unwilling to move for fear of someone noticing. Unwilling to reach out—unwilling to ask for help.

My mind races while my chest squeezes and constricts under the weight of my own hypocrisy. If they only knew the real me ...

The dull murmur of the instructor's voice guiding us through poses reminds me of the sweet yet biting vodka that immediately seared the sides of my throat and comforted my senses. With alcohol, my sharp tongue falls limply inside my mouth, and I feel no need to move or say anything, even if I disagree. I am afraid of my own voice. I am afraid of being misheard and misunderstood, so I always acquiesce. I drink to stave off the physical tremors as well as the authentic voice inside that screams at me to wake up. On my mat, in child's pose, my knowing self pounds behind my eyes like a hangover as I feign growth and self-awareness in a yoga class when I am actually a complete mess.

After twenty minutes of breathing stale alcohol, I can't play the charade any longer. I roll up my mat and excuse myself from class. I had never left a yoga class.

"I'm not feeling well," I lie. But I can't tell if it actually is a lie.

"Feel better." The other woman in class peeks at me from under her downward dog and shares a genuine, although upside down, smile. I realize I hadn't ever spoken to her, despite attending class with her almost every day. I recognize her pink hair tie and her sterling silver bracelets, her white tennis shoes at the foot of the stairs when I arrive, and her patterned tops with coordinated leggings. But I don't even know her name.

I smile back at her kindness and mouth, "See you tomorrow."

I've been attending this yoga class for almost a year, and I barely talk to anyone here. My mat is an island, and on normal days, I move perfectly through each pose, a model student, a model yogini.

Being an island is killing me slowly.

I walk into the bright, crisp sunshine and out to my car. The cold November air steals my breath, which would not even pass a driver's test. I keep hoping that enough sunlight, enough yoga, and enough positive thinking will cure me, will end this craving, and everything will return to normal. I crave belonging, but I hide my true self behind a veil of perfection.

Trying to be perfect is killing me.

My addiction has just seeped into my most sacred place—my yoga practice—and the acknowledgment feels like being buried while still alive. Soil dusts my belly and rolls into the crevices of my hips. One clump of heavy dirt lands on top of my chest, and the darkness rises, from hips, to belly, to chest, and eventually eyes. The space grows continually darker, smaller, and more suffocating.

My friend Cait drives up from Chicago to check on me. My sister had called Cait the previous night and told her how bad my drinking is. Then Cait texted everyone in our circle of six childhood friends, and so they all knew. I had slews of texts this morning: "Molly, you must do this for your kids." "Molly, I am here for you." "Molly, we love you."

Cait and I sit on my couch, and I debate whether or not I should cancel the appointment with the man who is coming over to fix the blinds. The blinds in Bennett's bedroom broke from overuse, so they hang diagonally across his window, and the disruptive angle drives me crazy. I nearly tore them off one afternoon until David came in and stopped me. He explained that they just needed a new string. He would call the number; could I be home Tuesday since he would be out of town on a trip? Yes. I stepped down from the chair I was using to reach the top of the blinds and agreed. My uselessness and incompetence filled the room like stale sea air as I walked by him and down the hall.

"Molly, this house is so sad. The heavy energy nearly knocked me over when I walked in the front door." Cait is right. The pain of a broken marriage and my own lost soul seeps through the freshly painted walls and perfect bamboo floorboards. My yard remains green and evenly mowed for the sake of the neighborhood. Forget that I finished a second bottle of wine in the garage last night while the kids played outside. At least there were no menacing dandelions popping up to tarnish the view. Until now, none of my friends knew, and I always planned to fix my drinking on my own, once my life settled down. For years I would start drinking around dinner time, but lately the opening of a bottle creeps closer and closer to mid-day, sometimes even morning. David is always on a trip, so I am free to open more bottles of wine after I put the boys to bed and continue until midnight when I finally pass out. The next day, I carefully place just enough bottles in the recycling bin so I don't draw attention, and I hide the rest inside paper grocery bags that I shove to the bottom of the garbage can.

But my sister knows. We drank the same. We were born thirteen months apart and had the same childhood, the same life. We are opposites in every way, but our drinking was always the same, like a slippery balm that soothed our exposure to life.

Cait tells me to cancel the appointment to fix the blinds and I do. Next, she wants to order lunch since I haven't eaten in days, but my stomach curls back at the mention of food. I take another sip of my water and try to think if I have any bottles of alcohol left hidden in the basement. Cait gets up and searches through my empty fridge and cupboards and comes back with a box of crackers and hummus.

"I'm so mad at David," she says and hands me a new LaCroix.

"You are?" I answer. "Why?"

Her statement genuinely baffles me. I have not considered David as being any part of this. David is like a hero to me. I'm the fuck-up. David is wildly successful and everyone in his job loves him. His company flies him to sought-out vacation spots and pays for him to stay in expensive hotels. Sometimes I went with him, but not lately. This wasn't always his job. When David and I met he was the company's claims manager, which meant he dealt with all the complaints and warranty issues. While dating, we joked about the stuff people found to submit a claim for. After a few company acquisitions, David worked his way up to Vice President of Sales, and we both thought all our problems were over.

"I think you should see a therapist." Cait is already searching for someone on her phone. "Where is David now?" she asks.

"He's in New York. It's a really important trip," I told her.

"It's not more important than you. This is an illness. You need medical help. You could lose your kids."

Cait points her phone at me with her right arm. The screen displays a website for a wellness clinic nearby and shows a woman's portrait next to a bio and all her credentials.

"I think you should call this woman."

The woman in the photo has a stylish short haircut and a colorful tattoo on her left forearm that sneaks out from the cuff of her blouse.

"You know, she looks cool and like she won't be all judgy." Cait throws a cracker in her mouth from the clump that fills her left fist.

I stare at Cait in awe as she logically and calmly formulates a plan. Her face reveals more freckles than when we were young kids, and I think I see a few gray hairs mingled among her thick, dark brown strands, but it also could be the sunlight that hits her high cheekbones and oval-shaped forehead. Cait has always been this way—abiding, courageous, and practical. But she also cries. And her tears have always given me permission to do the same. Is it possible this is not all my fault? Is it possible I am not only savable, but worth saving?

Cait looks up from her phone and into my eyes. She swallows.

Tears well up above her bottom lashes and overflow onto the tops of her speckled cheeks.

"Molly, you could have died. I had no idea, and I'm so sorry I wasn't here. But I'm here now."

Cait is so taken aback by the change in me that she operates a little too politely in the house at first, as if we are new acquaintances and not childhood best friends. She asks for things instead of opening cabinets and taking them on her own. The large and lonely space holds me hostage inside my addictive behavior. I wipe the crumbs from the coffee table and take Cait's plate. While she chews her last bite of crackers and hummus, I place the dish quietly into the sink and out of sight.

From the first time I pretended to drink a martini and smoke a cigarette on my Grandma's fencepost, I craved alcohol. At least, I craved the image of alcohol I saw from all the adults, TV shows, and magazines. Alcohol made people happy. When an adult had a bad day, they came home and poured a drink to make it better. I knew it worked. Upon taking the first sip, I watched their shoulders drop and the harsh creases in their faces soften. Halfway through the drink, I noticed their problems from just a minute ago were not so heavy; the person's entire demeanor lifted right along with the glass as they picked it up and floated uncaringly into the living room.

I knew I wanted that feeling and that power—the power to make all my troubles disappear and blur into the background of my mind. Sometimes I craved the drink to have fun. Celebrations and holidays seemed impossible without alcohol. I needed the buzz to hold a conversation and appear interesting. I needed just the right amount of dizziness in order to dance.

Sitting in my living room with Cait, my life in shambles, my body dying, my husband absent, I have to ask myself: *Where did I go wrong?* I knew my drinking had gotten out of control, but I didn't want to admit that I couldn't turn it around whenever I wanted, like taking a wrong turn off the highway and simply finding the next on-ramp.

In addition to my drinking becoming compulsive, I'm in the habit of speed reading several self-help books at a time. One sits on the coffee table, one on my nightstand, one in my bag in case I end up at the car wash or in a long pickup line at school. *Just don't sit still. Keep moving and you will figure this out.*

Not sitting still feeds my addiction. I chase but I can't catch the craving to be someone else or to disappear. Shame about my addiction heightens my desire to drink. Cait's words about my boys cut into my heart, and I think about what I have done. The other night I had driven home with them after having had several glasses of wine. When I understand what could have happened, fire spreads across my entire body, and I start to shake. I have no idea how to rid my body of the burning, gut-swirling sensations of shame other than to take a drink. I stand up and pace across the room, wondering if I still have any full bottles tucked away.

Cait's tenderness toward me baffles my senses. Since I am weak and shaky, she lovingly helps me tie my shoes in order to get into the car. She finds my purse, my keys, my jacket. I would be fine to drive, but she insists and nearly buckles my seatbelt for me after I reluctantly climb into the passenger side. The warmth of being taken care of like this calms the burning at my neck and makes my body somewhat limp like I have just been given permission to lie down in savasana.

Cait and I grab the boys from school and are outside playing with them when our friend Jen stops by. Cait and Jen sleep over that night, probably to safeguard me from booze, but their presence means everything to me. They left their own children, their husbands, and their responsibilities to stay with me. I've never felt so loved. Their presence is like an extra sweater I didn't even know I needed until someone pointed out I was shivering.

Theologian Nelle Morton uses the phrase "hearing into being," meaning we are able to recover lost pieces of ourselves when someone shares in our experience. Jen gives me a big hug when she sees me, and I can't tell whose shoulders are actually trembling—hers or mine. Our bodies shake like one, our pain and our fear collected and held by one body, one embrace.

Cait, Jen, and I, along with our other friends via phone, make a plan that I would start attending AA meetings. I make a therapy appointment with the woman with the arm tattoo. I tell myself I can do this, and I will. I am confident that if I can fix myself, if I can tackle my addiction, my eating disorder, and all the ways I cause harm to my own body, I can singlehandedly save my marriage. I will return to being the person David fell in love with.

When I make this choice, I have no idea that the healing and transformation is not for others, but for me. I have no idea that my body and the physical poses of yoga will grant me access to the deepest, darkest parts of my self, which will shape my character and increase my compassion.

That night, my exhausted body lies in bed, warm with friendship and hopeful with a supported plan. Cait turns out the small lamp near my bed and Jen brushes her teeth in the hall bathroom. At the same time I am being saved, David gets off an elevator in New York City. Later, he would tell me this was the spot of their first kiss.

KAPALABHATI : SKULL-SHINING BREATH

PART IV

Pranayama : Breath

LIFE FORCE

"How do you tell if something's alive?
You check for breathing."

—Markus Zusak

The fourth limb of yoga is pranayama, the practice of controlling our breath in order to awaken our life force (our energy) within. According to yoga philosophy, prana is both breath and life force, energy that moves continually and sustains every living thing. When prana ceases to exist, life ceases to exist.

Like asana, pranayama has physical benefits as well as emotional effects. Controlled breathing activates the parasympathetic nervous system, which counters the stress response and brings the body into balance. We feel calmer, clearer, and more at ease.

In addition to affecting the nervous system, our breath grants access to our intuition. It is through the breath that we are able to quiet the outside noise and distractions in order to go inside. This is how breath is used in yoga—as access to the true parts of self, rather than the illusions in the mind.

TWELVE

Seeking Answers and Seeking Strength

"Freedom is strangely ephemeral. It is something
like breathing; one only becomes acutely aware
of its importance when one is choking."

— George P. Shultz and William E. Simon

PRANA

IN TYLER'S YOGA CLASS, WE TRANSITION FROM WARRIOR ONE POSE INTO warrior two. I move from facing forward in a high lunge and open my body sideways. My arms glide from above my head to a T, and I bend further into my front leg. I find more ease in the sideways pose because I don't have to force my hips so square to the front. I now face the long glass doors of the yoga room and watch a few cars speed by on the weekday road. Right outside the window, the stone patio sits covered in leftover leaves. The tables and chairs of spring remain stored away, and while a few warm days have thawed the ground completely, the forecast calls for another snowstorm tonight.

"Inhale, then sink a little deeper as you exhale," offers Tyler.

I inhale and allow my chest to rise, then exhale out of an open mouth. I blow out loudly along with the other students in the room just as a small leaf whips up from the patio and makes a short loop into the air right above the ground. The leaf hangs for a second before it lands back on top of the other leaves. I smile because it looks as if I have just blown the leaf myself, like I have intentionally placed my lips right underneath its lightweight form and with my strong exhale forced the small leaf up and into the air. But that's impossible, right? I am inside a studio, behind panes of glass, and the leaf is outside on the cold ground. It's not impossible if you believe in prana, the life force that exists everywhere to move everything.

With my new therapist Alexa's permission, I decide to ask David outright if he is having an affair. No more hiding and seeking and trying to get passwords into his phone or email. I hadn't had a drink in two months, and I feel like a new person, like I could do anything. But my marriage is still horrible. If anything, sobriety illuminated more problems, whereas I thought it would fix everything. My body is stronger, muscles poke out that weren't there previously, and my skin is less swollen and blotchy. But my emotional self is still restless and quivering.

I come downstairs after putting the boys to bed, and I see David already sitting on the couch. My balance feels slippery in my wool socks, and I tighten my abdomen to make my way across the soft, wooden floor. The weight of my question hangs light and heavy at the same time, squeezing around my tongue and tingling on the edges of my lips. The minute my lungs flutter upward in anticipation that I might actually know the truth, my throat immediately closes around a heavy, wet blockage, something hard to swallow, if he actually answered, "Yes, I am having an affair."

I meditated all the days prior, and it occurred to me that I should just ask David instead of continuing my search to find evidence. I inhale as I sit next to him on the couch and reconsider whether or not to ask. He is right there. The ground as I know it is still under my feet. Maybe I should wait. Right now, I know my life. But once I ask the question, everything could change, and I'm not sure I want to hear David's answer.

Our nighttime ritual is watching a show on TV, physically near each other while also in two separate worlds. We engage in the same activity, but our experiences are wildly different. As a car commercial blinks loudly on the screen, David texts swiftly and deliberately on his phone. I watch him out of the corner of my eye and wonder how we got here, like adjacent fence posts sunk into the same soil, but the planks between us have long ago rotted and sagged precariously in the center. Still holding up, no one has the heart to say they are no longer into it.

"David," I begin. Inside, my stomach tightens. I sit up taller to stop myself from falling right into him. "David," I say again.

David looks up from his phone and says, "Yeah, what is it?"

I feel unsteady, and I want to reach out my hand and touch him or lean in close, something for support. I should stick it out longer, wait for everything to unfold, and more will be revealed. I want David to screw up. I want the life we have built to reveal its disintegrated center and crash down.

"Are you having an affair?" My question floats up and dangles there after it leaves my lips, so in the silence I add clarification. "It's OK if you are. I know we've had a rough year. And I just thought, if you are, then we could put it out there and deal with it, however we decide." I finish my speech and my plea.

David shifts his phone into his back pocket, unshaken. He places a hand on the side of his head and props his elbow on the edge of the couch.

"I would never do that to you." He smiles tenderly. "That's the one thing you never have to worry about, sweetie."

I sit still and search for any doubt in his eyes. But they glimmer with confidence and a little playfulness. His eyes say, *What a silly girl you are. What an absurd question.*

"OK," I respond after a long pause. His head still in his hand, he tilts it further to one side and pacifies me with a crooked grin. He makes no gesture or movement toward me. His phone beeps and he moves his hand to grab it, then leans his entire body back against the couch cushions in order to respond to the text. His eyes lower to the phone in his hands, and I am no longer in his gaze.

I get up and walk away for a glass of water. This silly accusation is all in my head, isn't it? At the kitchen sink, I fill my glass, and my head goes light and dizzy. My feet are solid on the cold tile floor, and I watch the predicted snowfall that has started outside our small kitchen window. I gulp down the water and feel no further along than before, until a voice enters my mind and says emphatically: *Molly, if you ever find out he just lied to you, you're leaving.*

A few days later I sit on the floor at the foot of my bed and review the instructions from my meditation book. "Breath of Fire," I read, and I am immediately brought back to the dimly lit yoga space from college and the pranayamas we had learned. I had completely forgotten about that teacher and that class until now. I had completely forgotten that I even attended yoga classes for an entire semester in college, and that I saved my limited income to pay for the classes instead of going out to the bars with my friends. I completely forgot about the reddish-colored carpet and soft orange lamps, the presence and connection I experienced with a small group of students that year. Yoga has been with me for a long time, and I can't believe I forgot.

Comforted and surprised by the memory, I bend my thumbs into my palms and curl my four fingers around them. Seated cross-legged on the floor of my bedroom, I sense the comforter flopped over behind me, inches away from my straight spine. I extend and raise my arms up to shoulder height and bend my elbows to make a goal post. I hold my hands in the intentional fist position and close my eyes. I imagine the side curtain on the doorway and the tiny glowing apartments outside black windows. I smell the earthy incense and try to recall the instructor's name and her hair. I see long, curly strands and a narrow face, and I realize she was probably about the same age I am now.

I inhale deeply in order to prepare for breath of fire.

Originally, I had flipped to the index of my new meditation book to search for the word addiction. But just below it I read the word anger, and I curiously flipped to that page instead. The book has different meditations designed to heal different problems, like illnesses, anxieties, and closed hearts.

I hadn't thought that I might be angry, angry at David and angry at myself. But thinking about it now, anger makes sense. When uncomfortable thoughts or feelings arise, they explode in the form of impatience with my boys or yelling at my husband. Often, I even yell at myself, my habits, my eating, my lack of exercise, the fact that the bathroom sink always gets clogged. All this blaming, violent self-talk, just to avoid the admission that I might be angry.

Before starting the pranayama, I enact the fifth niyama, ishvara pranidhana, and say a prayer: *God, I surrender my anger to you. I surrender my resentment and my pain for all I have done and for all that has been done to me. Take it. Please, take it.*

With my arms like goal posts and my fingers curled into fists like the picture shown, I begin breath of fire. I force a gust of fiery air out my open mouth. The ball of heat cannons off the edge of my tongue and stings the insides of my lips. I plunge my stomach inward toward my spine until it practically reaches the comforter behind me. I wriggle my sits bones further into the carpet as if digging my body into sand. I press my thumbs to the insides of my palms and squeeze them in place with the rest of my fingers. The fast inhale arrives like a wave through my nose, and the equal exhale rushes out like the inevitable tide.

Exhale, inhale, exhale, inhale, exhale, inhale, exhale, inhale, exhale.

I pause to catch my breath. Breath of fire feels like losing breath instead of absorbing it. I expel negative energy and hold my fists strong, but the inhale that comes after never feels like enough. My bicep muscles tire after one minute, so I drop my hands and place them onto my belly. I inhale more slowly and feel my stomach expand. I release my jaw, and as I exhale, my navel yanks back toward my spine. I push out the exhale like a dragon breathing fire. The flames hit the open air of my bedroom and flutter the hemlines of the curtains that move above churning heat vents.

My pain body emerges and everything I have ever been angry about, everything I have ever propped up seems to crash and arrive at the same speed as my breath.

Can I forgive my childhood?

Inhale.

Can I forgive my mothering now that I have my own children?

Exhale.

Can I forgive the image I had in my head of what my life would look like and the complete detour that it actually is?

Inhale.

Can I forgive my addiction and know this is part of my path?

Exhale
Can I forgive myself for not being perfect?
Inhale
A new thought arrives.
Is this all my fault?
Exhale

SANSANGASANA : RABBIT POSE

PART V

Pratyahara : Presence

CONTROLLING AHARA
(WITHDRAWAL OF THE SENSES)

"The genius of yoga practice is that it cultivates
the capacity to experience a close-range, moment-
by-moment inspection of reality. In fact, yoga
teaches that living fully in the moment is the only
doorway into the hidden realities of the self."

—Stephen Cope

To practice pratyahara, the fifth limb of yoga, we withdraw from outside sensations. We eliminate noise and perception in order to become aware of what is true and real. Pratyahara is the practice of presence, and it asks us to go inside, to remove the lure of external or internal distraction so we can pay attention to self.

We all lead very busy lives, which undermines presence and takes our focus out in many different directions. Rather than remove the outside sensations, as Pratyahara suggests, we engage relentlessly in everything that is outside ourself, feeding the distraction instead of what actually needs attention. As women, we spend a lot of time focused on others, a form of self-refusal masked as caregiving. I love staying busy around my children and the home because then I don't have to sit still with my own emotions.

Ahara is the part of us that keeps us unaware of our true self. It is the conscious, rational part of us that is not pure awareness. The first four limbs all contain tools for restraining the senses, which then lead us to a practice of introversion, to pratyahara. The yamas and niyamas teach us about our character and how we want to behave. Asana and pranayama attend to the body, to our stories and our emotional self. Pratyahara asks us to feel and witness the present moment so we can distinguish illusion from truth and distraction from awareness. Pratyahara invites us to stop running and begs us to attend to ourself.

THIRTEEN

Closed and Opening

"And so the prayer narrowed itself down to that
simple entreaty—Please tell me what to do—repeated
again and again. I don't know how many times I
begged. I only know I begged like someone pleading
for her life, and the crying went on forever."

—Elizabeth Gilbert

SANSANGASANA AND MATSYASANA

I AM ALREADY ON MY KNEES AND I LIKE IT HERE. I FLEX MY TOES UNDER my body weight as my butt sits heavily on my heels. We breathe in broken toe pose, a backward direction for the toes that creates a much needed stretch. I find comfort in the unusual orientation and in the tolerance.

"We're going to move into rabbit pose," Tyler says. "Pay attention to where you are. Before moving, let's inhale."

I release the stretch of broken toe pose and fold the tops of my feet under to prepare for sansangasana (rabbit pose). I still sit on my heels, knees bent, hands on top of thighs, and spine erect. On each inhale, my chest lifts and my crown reaches skyward; on each exhale, my tailbone grounds further onto my heels. Rabbit is an inversion. I move my hands from my thighs and place them around my back in order to hang on to my heels. I bend my torso forward and place the crown of my head—the very top—onto my mat in front of me. As I fold over to place my head on the floor, my hips naturally lift off my heels. I let them rise as high as they want while gripping onto my heels for traction. The more I pull and the higher I lift my hips, the more my throat closes as my body inverts. Eventually, my chin presses sharply against my chest, which almost completely blocks the airway. The lack of space in my throat creates a fullness and a comfort, like a weighted blanket being placed on my body until I can't move.

Even though I constantly kept house, I hired Maria to come clean once a month. Throughout each day, I wiped off counters, picked up toys, washed dishes, and put away clothes, but Maria came to do the deep work underneath, the cleaning that always got overlooked. She vacuumed the carpet in my office, dusted base boards, and shook out rugs and curtains. Unlike Maria, I spent my time on the very surface. I remained busy and put on a sparkling appearance for visitors while she dove deep into the dirty crevices of our home, the spaces beneath what guests usually see.

As you go through someone's home, dusting, adjusting, and putting things in their place, it's easy to eavesdrop, to notice objects, and discover secrets, even if you try not to. I always admired Maria for being the very best at her job. She insisted on bringing her own mop to all her homes, like a carpenter with his own tools or a writer with her favorite pen. While cleaning, Maria stayed focused on her task. She dusted without looking at the crack in the frame and wondering how it got there. She moved stacks of books and then put them back without reading the titles. She picked up a pair of pants off the bedroom floor and wasn't the least bit curious about the receipt that fell out.

But after cleaning someone's home for five years, sweeping up crumbs and cobwebs, it's impossible not to see and touch things or have them touch you. It's impossible not to let your senses pick up on the dirt and mildew as you go. Unlike a random visitor, it's impossible for someone like Maria not to see the truth.

I knew Maria would notice the new hole in the drywall where the dining chair got thrown. Then she would remember the year before when she came and found the bedroom door handle cracked and broken from when someone tried to forcefully break in.

I remember sitting on my bed, hearing the pounding and screaming, the splitting wood and bending metal as the lock cracked inside the door frame. I wondered if I should get up and turn the handle. But I sat with my legs bent to my chest and my forehead to my knees, huddled like a bunny, too afraid to actually move.

One time, after Maria left, I walked into my closet and found a nearly empty bottle of wine propped up next to one of my cowboy boots. I must have left the bottle hidden in there under my long dresses, and Maria discovered it while straightening my shoes. Maria rarely took anything out of a room or threw anything away. If there was a pile of old papers somewhere, she'd move them only to wipe off the surface underneath, then neatly stack them back in order. Seeing the bottle, I could picture her finding it, dutifully dusting it off, and leaving it almost in the exact same spot. Maybe setting the bottle there, in my eyesight, was an invitation, like a concerned hand on my shoulder. I could hear Maria's gentle voice asking me, "Molly, are you OK?"

"If you feel some adrenaline while in rabbit pose, like you're in fight or flight mode, that's completely normal," says Tyler. "It happens when you close your thyroid in the posture."

We are huddled over like bunnies, crowns pressed to the floor. I am curious about Tyler's warning because I feel completely safe in this locked throat position. My breath makes a raspy sound each time I inhale and exhale, and my inability to move or to make any noise comforts me. I am protected from everything outside. All my senses—touch, taste, smell, sight, and sound—are tucked in tightly, like my chin that presses firmly into my chest. I rock back and forth on the crown of my head, and observe the hollowed silence.

I relish being in sansangasana, curled up neatly like a bunny, thyroid and throat closed, unable to speak. My upper back and shoulders stretch and the muscles pull down and out from my spine. I increase the lengthening sensation and pull harder with my hands on my heels. I picture stretches of ligaments expanding like rubber bands underneath my skin.

After several minutes in rabbit, Tyler reminds us there is a counter pose—fish pose. I haven't done or thought about matsyasana (fish pose) for years, since learning the pose from my mom in our living room. My first time doing fish pose felt so completely against any instinct in my body. My mom instructed me to lie on my back, lift up on my forearms in order to puff out my chest, and crane my neck backward to place the crown of my head on the floor behind me. Fish pose is the opposite of tucking in your chin; instead, you flip your neck the other direction, opening and exposing your entire throat to the sky.

I trusted my mom, and we moved into the pose together. We arched up like fish on the living room floor, flung our heads back onto the carpet and opened our eyes wide to the upside-down room behind us. We stayed there for several minutes, and after that day, we always ended our afternoon practice in fish pose. Not many of my teachers have incorporated matsyasana into a yoga sequence since.

Now that Tyler has given us permission to take fish pose as a class, I am brought back. I smell the antique, scratchy rug in my old living room. I see the wood paneling that framed out the white, crackled ceiling. My throat tingles, and I recall the stretching sensation of my skin across my windpipe.

I flip over onto my back, extend my legs, and place my palms face down right under my hips. I press my forearms into the mat for support, and lift up my chest. I engage my neck muscles to reach my head up and back and place my crown on the mat, this time the opposite way from rabbit pose. Instead of closing my throat, I open it. Instead of hiding, I arch back like a daring fish who flips itself momentarily out of the surface of the water.

I don't feel completely comfortable in the extremely open position of my heart and throat, but I tolerate it. Once again, I am brought to a calm stillness in my mind, like a fish cradled inside the depths of the ocean, unaffected by the muffled vibrations of life above.

It's unrealistic to think that in order to practice pratyahara, we need to find a moment of complete silence without the pull of kids, home, pets, or work. We are bombarded by input every day, and the more input coming in, the more we are lured to the artificial surface of life and away from our true, wise self. Pratyahara asks us to stay and can be practiced in the midst of chaos. Stay, pause, breathe, and release the expectation of the perfect yoga practice or the perfect home. Make time to attend to yourself, even when remaining still is uncomfortable.

While Maria dusted screens with an old washcloth, I kept busy typing on my computer. Her oldest daughter pushed Andrew on the swing in the backyard, and our other kids waited their turn. Maria came into the kitchen and asked me about the new hole in the wall behind the dining table. I looked up from my computer and glanced over at my poor patch job.

"We had another fight."

Maria nodded silently.

She looked to the left of my laptop and saw my wedding rings sitting on the table. I had taken them off while typing. Maria held eye contact with me for a little too long, and I looked out the window to see Andrew now dismounting from the swing and Bennett trying to help young Anna on.

Once Maria allowed the awareness to enter her senses, it was impossible to look away. The truth was on the bathroom tiles and inside the bedsheets. She saw it while mopping the floors, putting away silverware, and folding the children's pajamas neatly on their beds.

I finished feeding all five kids a snack as Maria packed up her things to leave. As always, she handed me the tied-up bag of dirty towels to wash, and I handed her the monthly payment in cash. We hugged goodbye.

"OK, Molly, you are strong. I'll see you next time."

In December that year, I left Maria her payment plus extra. I set the envelope on the desk near the front door before taking the boys to school and going to work. I also left a card: "Maria, I don't know what I'd do without you. Thank you and Merry Christmas! All my love, Molly"

When I returned home from work, there was a card with my name on it, where my envelope had been: "Molly, you are so brave, and we appreciate you very much. Merry Christmas! We love you! Maria, Alberto, Lily, Carmen, and Anna."

I didn't feel brave. I felt fake, like I wanted to tuck myself into rabbit pose and never face the sky. I never wanted to leave this house or its secrets. I never wanted to expose my throat or my hiding places. I felt silly and entitled. Maria was brave. Maria worked in other people's homes in a country that didn't recognize her as a citizen. Yet she lived here and drove here and risked herself every day for her children. Yet Maria knew me, and I trusted her completely, which is why I let her clean my house and why I also loved her so much. So if Maria told me I was brave, maybe I was.

In fish pose I breathe into the openness. I let the skin of my throat stretch until it feels like I might rip completely open, but I never do. And when I lower out of the pose by tucking my chin first and then dropping off of my forearms and elbows, I lie on my back and pant with relief. My breath has much more space than before. I close my eyes and smile at the swirling aliveness right at the center of my throat. This is freedom: I can say and do anything I want.

I walked upstairs after reading Maria's note and went to my secret hiding spot. I pulled open the middle bathroom drawer that no one used. Two bright pink Post-it notes I had placed there read:

You are brave.

You are enough.

FOURTEEN

A Journey into Presence

"Maybe journey is not so much a journey ahead, or a
journey into space, but a journey into presence."

—Nelle Morton

BAKASANA

SUN SHINES UNIFORMLY ON THE PATCH OF GREEN GRASS CENTERED inside the rectangular courtyard. Carefully chosen flowers and manicured shrubs outline the edges, and small vines climb gracefully up low stone walls. My yoga mat feels bumpy and lumpy under my bare feet, different outside than on the even wooden surface of the yoga studio.

The weekly farmers' market buzzes on the sidewalk just outside the courtyard. I hear glass jars of homemade salsa clinking together and the rustling of long-stemmed sunflowers being shoved into stiff paper bags.

Our instructor Andrea moves us into goddess pose, then malasana, a low, wide-legged squat, in order to set up for an arm balance pose, bakasana, which means crow. From the squatting position I am in, I place both hands on the mat between my legs, and begin to waddle each knee as high onto the backs of my forearms as possible. I bend my elbows even further and gently lift one heel and then the other off the ground. My forearms press against my shins to make the rest of my body float upward. I rise onto my tiptoes, now barely touching the ground, and my arms begin to jostle under my body's entire weight.

"Don't look down," advises Andrea. "Look straight ahead and lift your chin."

I want to keep looking down. David had recently been on a business trip to Las Vegas, and I hadn't heard from him the entire day. The boys watched a movie on the couch, probably *Finding Nemo*, and the sun had almost disappeared from the sky. A faint, pink glow remained just above the neighbor's roof as I looked over the tops of the boys' heads, across the living room, and out the large window. I wondered when David would call. I kept trying to reach him, but there was no answer. It's Vegas, so he could have been busy, drunk, in trouble. Or all three.

Our living room was an addition to the original home. The previous owner was a divorced woman who met her second husband when she was a flight attendant and he was a pilot for United. When he moved in, I'm told they had a beautiful wedding ceremony on their newly built patio, part of the remodeling they did on the entire house. David and I bought the home when the owners' two daughters were going to college. It had just the right number of bedrooms and the perfect layout for raising teenagers. David and I planned to stay at least until the boys were through high school.

I stare at my arms in crow. My head is bent completely down in the balance pose, to the point that my chin almost touches my chest. With my head down, I can see each of my toes floating above the mat and my fingertips peek out from under my shoulders. I feel the strength of holding myself up while still being able to measure how close I am to the ground below.

Andrea repeats her direction to lift our gaze. I steady my arms by pressing fully into my palms and bending further into my forearms. I pull my abdominals in and start to raise my chin. I center my gaze on the edge of the flower bed in front of me. The blades of green grass appear longer from this viewpoint, and I notice a butterfly land on one of the rose bushes. I feel my arms sink and my body land into the sweet spot of the balance pose.

The night I couldn't get hold of David, I was restless. I wanted to run out and buy a bottle of wine. I even made up a lie in my head that I would tell the boys—I needed dish soap or gas, and I would only be gone for a few minutes. I could stash the bottle under the bar cabinets and hide the wine in my coffee mug like I had done so many times before. I'd have a wonderful evening with myself after I put the boys to bed, and I wouldn't have to worry about where my husband was or what he was doing.

I stood with my hands on my hips and stared at the bar I had grown to hate. My safe haven had become my demon, and I despised every inch of the marble countertop, the frosted glass cabinets, and the tall leather stools. I remembered an image of a kitchen with open shelving. I walked over to the cabinets and opened one of the doors. Tall clear glasses lined up perfectly on the shelf behind it. I examined the hinges and went to the garage to get the screwdriver.

"Mommy, what are you doing?" Bennett asked from the couch as he turned his head back and saw me climbing down from the counter with one of the cabinet doors in my hands.

"I'm taking these doors off. It will look nicer."

Andrew was looking now, too, but then they both said nothing and turned their attention back to the movie.

I checked my phone. Still no call or text from David.

Once the doors were off the cabinets and the glasses had all been removed, I started wandering around the house, looking for books and frames and things that looked like they should be displayed on open shelving. I remembered the photo I had seen online and grabbed the hand-painted vase someone had given to us as a wedding present. Once I had collected enough items, I began to arrange them on the shelves. I stayed busy so I wouldn't think about alcohol. I stayed busy so I wouldn't think about David in Las Vegas.

I moved the stack of cookbooks I had arranged to the lower shelf so I could reach them more easily. Plus, the silver decorative bowls looked better on the upper shelf. I would have to get the sculpture of the fish I made in college back from my parent's house because it would look great as part of this new display. I left room for the sculpture and stood back to admire my work.

"Boys! Look what I did to the bar!"

I checked my phone. David still hadn't called.

The therapist whom Cait and I chose during our online search was good. At my first appointment I opened by telling her something was broken in my marriage but I didn't know what. I told her I wanted to quit drinking. And I figured if we could get to the bottom of what was wrong with me and what I could change, it would be a good start. My therapist, Alexa, smiled, and her eyes squinted slightly above her raised cheeks. The colorful tattoo on her arm was of a butterfly, and she sat on a stool that had a rubber ball at the bottom instead of legs, so it kind of rocked and rolled as she moved and talked. I liked her a lot. I went to see her for an hour every week, and even when I arrived thinking I had nothing to say, we ended up talking the entire time. By the time I left, I was lighter and more accepting, like a petal that becomes ready to fall from its stem in a moment of surrender.

The more I saw her, the more I had to say.

My therapist said I could always call her to make a same-day appointment in the event of an emergency. I took note of her suggestion but wasn't sure what kind of situation would require that I get in to see her immediately, especially since I already had a standing appointment each week.

Now steady in crow pose, my gaze travels evenly across the tips of grass, and I glance up even further to see if the butterfly is still on the rosebush. As soon as I do, I know I've gone too far. Now beyond a comfortable balance,

I feel my weight continue forward, which places too much pressure on my wrists. Unable to undo my tightly positioned arms and legs in time, I lurch all the way downward, and hard dirt smacks sharply against my chin.

For a moment, I am suspended in air like petals blowing off a plant in the wind before they land. As I begin to fall out of the balance, my body rises slightly at first, and I briefly try to catch myself. There is a weightlessness and freedom in the in-between as I float momentarily from steady balance to a stinging fall.

I lay there in the grass and pause before untangling my sore body and moving to recover in child's pose on my mat. My chin burns, and I check it for blood.

CATUR SVANASANA

"From child's pose, move into dolphin," says Cassie. I received an email today about an advanced yoga class being offered in the town nearby, so I adjust my plans and make sure to attend. I am in the mood to push my body, to sweat and shake, and maybe even scream. I can't handle another child's pose or savasana that forces me to be alone with my thoughts and inner voices.

I crave the physical exertion. Cassie cues the poses by name and does less demonstration, so we move quickly and are expected to know where to put our limbs when we hear the Sanskrit name. The class provides space for my own practice with minimal instruction. I test my yoga skills, and I trust my body. I need to feel my strength today.

Catur svanasana (dolphin pose) is downward dog on your forearms instead of your hands. I take a deep inhale, and my belly expands. I exhale and press my forearms and palms firmly onto the mat and tuck my toes. I pull in my abdominals and float my knees off the mat. I continue the exhale as I lift my hips and straighten my legs, now completely supported on my forearms. My knees remain slightly bent as I inhale again, exhale, and lower my heels closer to the ground while reaching my hips back and upward. I want to keep my forearms on the mat while also pressing firmly into the balls of my feet, which allows my shoulders to spread open and my spine to lengthen. I inhale, aware of the strength of my forearms and my biceps. I look at the definition in my shoulders and lift out of them even more. I remember my yoga instructor's suggestion in college and roll my shoulders back and down, away from my ears. The small adjustment pushes my hips up higher, lengthens my spine, and my heels finally reach the ground.

From dolphin, we move into pincha mayurasana (forearm stand), an inverted balance like handstand, except our forearms are on the mat instead of our hands. I have never done this pose, but I am eager to try. I carefully watched Cassie when she demonstrated the pose a few minutes before. She kept her shoulders strong and forearms firmly pressed, while using only her core to very slowly lift her legs, until they were completely vertical above her torso.

Moving from dolphin into forearm stand requires an amount of trust in my body I am not used to. I trust my hands and their ability to hold me in a handstand. I trust my core and my quads and know how to drop down out of handstand gracefully without kicking too far and toppling over the back of my body.

In forearm stand, I'm more vulnerable. I am forced to be in alignment without faking it. I kick up and let my heels search for the wall behind me. I hit it, which makes a single thud, and I exhale relief. With my feet grazing the wall for stability, I press into my forearms and rise up a little more out of my shoulders.

"Keep looking ahead," Cassie coaxes.

I stare at my fingertips, straight and together like fins. I feel the tender skin of my forearms pinch slightly against the rubber of my yoga mat. All my weight on that skin, the soft and sensitive part underneath my arms that never sees the sun. As my body lifts, it almost floats directly above my shoulders, and I can feel the sensation when I actually arrive at vertical. I slowly remove one foot away from the security of the wall, and then the other. Cassie becomes silent, but I can feel her body near mine, watching.

I am upside down, yet floating. My legs and torso feel weightless, and I flatten my forearms fully onto the mat for support. My shoulder muscles ripple silently, which tells me they are strong enough to support me.

Cassie finally speaks, "You got it, Molly." Her voice is soft and centered, but in my head it sounds like grand applause.

FIFTEEN

Independence Day

"At various points in our lives, or on a quest, and
for reasons that often remain obscure, we are
driven to make decisions which prove with
hindsight to be loaded with meaning."

—Sri Swami Satchidananda

PHALAKASANA

It's the morning of the Fourth of July. Music blasts from the portable speaker as I approach my eighth sun salutation. My plan is to complete fifteen total salutations while moving through various poses in between—utkatasana, virabadhrasana, trikonasana. I am in the mirrored workout room in our basement, fighting to stay sober and sane. I haven't had a drink since February, and I thought my marriage would have improved by now. Without alcohol to tune out, I find my awareness expanding and my list of resentments long, beyond the inequity and suffocation of my existing marriage. I think back to my Grandma's boyfriend, an old man who loved to have me sit on his lap and kiss him. I hated his stench of aftershave and cigarettes and his constantly prickly cheeks and chin, but I never considered that I might have a choice in the matter. Other questionable memories, which had been drowned by wine and cocktails, float up, like sunken gold from a ship lost at sea, and I feel I am reliving all the oppressive behaviors imposed on me by men—the enticement, capture, imprisonment, and the reforming of a woman's identity.

I thought I was saving everyone and that when I quit drinking, I would be able to love David better, more securely. But David seems as distant as ever, and he still travels all the time. We don't have sex. We talk, and he always reassures me everything is fine, but I feel so unsettled.

Exercise helps. I command myself to do little triceps pushups while in plank pose before flowing comfortably into downward facing dog.

The upbeat music carries me along like a dolphin in an ocean's wave; vibrations fill my body as I match my breath with each shift in movement. Some days I need the loud music. Some days, especially when practicing yoga by myself and under my own instruction, I need the motivation to keep going. No one is here watching me. I am the only one keeping myself accountable. A song comes on that is too slow for my senses, so I click to the right to hear the next track on my playlist.

I arrive in phalakasana (plank pose) and hold myself there for several deep breaths. I glance at my abdominals in the mirror and notice they are flat and strong. They have been changing after all this yoga and no booze. The weak and sagging skin after having babies is noticeably tightening and wrapping back together. The stretch marks and extra folds are still there, but the skin doesn't hang down as low. The progress makes me proud, like an athlete finally starting to see the results of her training.

A good song comes on and I smile. The movement and music are doing the trick to get me out of my funk. I open my body out to side plank and stretch my left arm up to the ceiling. My right obliques harden into action. Today is going to be a good day, I think. I feel excited and sweaty and ready to celebrate the Fourth of July with the kids. I flip back down to plank and rotate my body to the opposite side in order to work all muscles evenly.

The boys have been chattering away about the fireworks over the lake later tonight. Sparklers—I text David and remind him to buy sparklers.

David has taken the boys to the store for summer cookout supplies— hamburger meat, condiments, pasta salad. I mention on their way out the door that watermelon sounds good and that it would be easy to transport to my parents' house and down to the lake. Always an easy crowd pleaser.

After the last sun salutation, I go upstairs to get a glass of water. I check the time. I'll be able to shower and change before everyone gets home. I start to walk upstairs, but my phone rings. It's my friend Sam, so I answer, pausing on the steps and turning back toward the kitchen.

"Hey, Sam! Happy Fourth!"

"I found everything. I haven't slept all night." Her voice almost whispers and shakes. I have trouble hearing her words, and I also have no idea what she is talking about.

She cries, loudly now. "Tom has a girlfriend. It's been at least ten years. I went into his phone and found everything last night."

"What?" I said. "Oh my God! Sam, I'm sorry. How do you know?"

Sam explains how she woke up in the middle of the night and entered Tom's password, the one she had watched him enter one day and memorized until she wrote it down. She waited until he was asleep, just as planned, and once in his phone, all the truth was there and so obvious— texts, emails, photos, everything.

Sam is at her in-laws' lakehouse for the holiday and hasn't let anyone know. I can't imagine anything worse.

I take a long drink of water at the sink and refill my glass. The phone is wedged between my ear and my shoulder and as Sam talks, her voice starts to trail off. My stomach knots up, and without meaning to, I stop paying attention.

"Sam," I interrupt. "I'm really sorry, but I have to call you right back." My voice is firm, and Sam simply says, "OK, no problem."

I let the phone drop onto the couch as I walk into David's office. While the kids and David are gone, I have a limited window of opportunity.

I see David's iPad sitting on his desk. I haven't searched for anything for a while, part of my giving up and letting go.

I look around self-consciously, even though I know no one is home. Like a child sneaking an extra cookie, I grab the iPad and come out to sit on the couch.

I click on the icon of a white envelope, David's hotmail account. To my surprise, it opens right up. Usually I am blocked at this point, locked out of everything, and unable to look further without a password. My stomach jolts with giddiness, and I scan the screen for clues. His inbox is empty. David never uses this email account. I click on trash. I see offers and scams, but my eyes go quickly to an email from someone named Nicole Weston.

I recognize this name, but I don't know her. I saw David texting her while we were at Andrew's kindergarten performance last fall, right? I have also seen her comment a few times on David's Facebook posts, and I thought I saw him texting her one day when we were waiting to pick up the boys from school. But David texts a lot of people from work, and his phone is his main way of communicating. David and Nicole work together—that's it.

I open the email from Nicole Weston. And a bomb goes off.

The room becomes completely silent, more silent than the already empty house. It is a deafening silence, where no sounds can be heard at all—not the neighbor's lawnmower, not the kids playing basketball in the driveway, not the birds dipping into the feeder in the garden. I read, and silent darkness envelops me. A black circle closes in around my body. Flashes of light illuminate the words on the white screen, and I see what I had known all along. Her words. To him. Her sweet words.

"I want all of you."

"I love you, but how can this work?"

"I fake it for my husband, but I can't tell him. He is too sweet."

As I continue reading, my world starts crumbling. Yet I still have to read everything twice, and slowly.

Towers come crashing down around me. Pieces of my future slowly sink away into groundlessness, one by one. Reality as I knew it becomes empty. Still, I question myself. Wait, who is writing this letter? Is this my letter? And who is the letter meant for? Why is someone writing to my husband like this?

Reading the love letter, I think this woman seems a lot like me. Maybe that's it; maybe this letter to David is actually from me. Maybe I wrote this letter a while ago and just don't remember doing it. There are sweet words. The woman who wrote this needs him. She wants him. She wrote about starting her business. I had a business. Maybe this letter was from me.

But then there is crying, and begging, and pathetic pleading. This woman seems like a heartsick fifteen-year-old writing to her high school crush in her diary. She seems lost and confused. She hates her husband, and she is desperately in love with mine.

After a third or fourth read, I realize this letter is not from me.

The black text of the email blurs on the glowing screen. I throw the iPad aside onto the couch like a hot pan. Instinctively, I jump up and run for the garage. I get in the car, turn the key, and back out of the driveway. I drive and try to get as far away from the iPad—and from my life—as possible. The only thing I have with me is my phone. I turn the radio on and then off. My sweaty palms slip on the steering wheel, and my right foot shakes under the extraordinary effort it takes to simply press down on the gas pedal. Then I remember my friend and call Sam back.

She answers right away.

"David has been having an affair. I just found the emails. He's had a girlfriend since at least last year." My hands find their grip on the steering wheel. "I don't know what to do. I can't believe it."

Sam was silent.

"I can't believe it." Sam repeats. "Oh, my God. You knew, Molly. You knew. What are you going to do?"

"I don't know. What are you going to do?"

"I don't know."

Driving on the highway to nowhere, I finally come to. I feel exhilarated and devastated all at the same time. I was right.

Then I remember the iPad back on the couch, the boys, the grocery store, and the Fourth of July. Maybe I should be doing something else? Maybe I should be searching for more evidence. What if David and the boys are home by now? Would he wonder where I went? Would he see the iPad and know what I found? I am running like I always do. Nothing makes sense.

The voice in my head booms: *Molly, get your shit together and go back there. There will be plenty of time to freak out later.*

I turn the car around and drive back to the house. When I pull into the garage, David's car isn't there. They aren't back yet. He doesn't know I know.

I run into the house and grab the iPad from the couch. I put it carefully back in David's office, on the desk, just as I found it.

Then I go back to it and re-read her words. They are still there, so easy for me to read. Everything I feared is true in one, giant, collapsing moment.

I do one more self-punishing read before forwarding all the emails to my own account. I set the iPad back down and go upstairs to take a shower. The warm water runs down my body like a cleansing rain. I wrap my arms around my neck and back in order to hold onto myself. I let the steady stream rinse everything away. Once clean, I get dressed. I put on my swimsuit, cut off shorts, and a red-and-white striped shirt.

I walk downstairs and hear David's car pulling into the garage. Little voices and plastic grocery bags rustle enthusiastically as the boys come tripping into the house with their purchases.

"Hi, Mommy! We got sparklers!" The boys yelp.

"I bought you shrimp!" David exclaims, so proud of himself. David doesn't like shrimp, but he knows I do.

"I thought we could make it for dinner one night this week." David sets the bags on the counter and goes back out to get some more.

I stand there, unable to move or help. Dinner? This week? His words are out of place. What about the woman? What about Nicole Weston, the person you love?

The man is buying me shrimp and talking about dinner in a few days. It's as if he has no idea what is actually going on. But he does know, right? Since he is the one doing it? For a moment in time I see everything. I see his behavior and actions within his orchestrated world. I see a world created and controlled by him where I have been dutifully playing along. While I am trying to save my marriage, David is in another relationship. It is like casting a line in an extinct sea. I am too late.

When I called my therapist's number for an emergency appointment, her receptionist scheduled me right on that same day, just as promised. I entered Alexa's office and blurted out "David has been having an affair" before she even had a chance to sit down on her stool. She took a deep breath and waited.

"I was right!!!" I almost yelled.

"You were right!" Alexa repeated and her arms went up into the air like in celebration.

She lowered her arms and motioned for me to join her in a deep inhale. We both exhaled collective breaths of reassurance as we sat down to talk.

Alexa took another deep inhale and slow exhale before speaking. Our excitement about my intuition being proven correct was met with the tenderness of reality, that David had been cheating, lying, and my search had ended with the brutal truth of it all.

"Does David know? What was his reaction?" Alexa asked gently.

I help David put away the shrimp he bought for me along with the other groceries. I debate whether to bring it up or just go on with the Fourth of

July holiday as if I don't know. For the sake of the kids and my family's party, maybe the truth can wait. After all, I've gone this long without even knowing. But while the boys play outside with the neighbors, I have a moment alone with David.

"I know about Nicole." I watch David's face for his reaction and bite down on the inside of my lip. I have a tendency to smirk when I am uncomfortable, so if I bite hard enough on my mouth, the pain reminds me to stay serious.

"It's not what you think," replies David.

"I found the emails. They are pretty explicit."

David stands silent.

"You just broke us." I say in a half-cry while shaking my head at him.

"I did?" David's voice cracks, which I never heard before. His eyes fill with tears, and the tops of his cheeks flush bright red. He rubs his temples and sits down in a chair at the kitchen table across from me.

"No. No. I didn't break us. It's not what you think."

"I would've done anything for you. I would've followed you anywhere."

"No," David repeats and shakes his own head, now completely forlorn.

"Do you love her? In the emails, she says she loves you."

"Yes, I love her. But I don't want to lose you, lose us."

I sit and think for a second, considering his honest statement.

"But I want to be married to someone who loves me." My words hang in the air like a ripe rose petal floating gently in the wind before landing on solid ground below, one final indication of its existence. This is my truth and my admission: I want to be loved. And I am no longer ashamed to admit it, no longer willing to accept anything less.

Alexa listened as I recapped the last two days and my waves of emotions. One moment I rose, elated that I knew the truth, and the next I fell, terrified about what to do. Then I crashed even further down into despair as I let my husband's love for another woman sink into my bones. My skin felt hot and wet, like a damp towel that provided protection and warmth but also a heavy chill.

Alexa tasked me to be a witness for the next few weeks.

"Try to remain present and observe. It will teach you a lot about David's intentions and his character. When the time comes, you will know what to do. Now at least you know you can trust yourself."

The gift of presence and paying attention does not mean we get the answers we want to hear. But presence will always lead us to truth.

I left Alexa's office defeated, knowing that because of this reality, no matter what choice I made, nothing going forward would be easy or ever the same.

SIXTEEN

Breaking Open

"I don't think you go low just to stay there, or
to be punished. I think you go low in order
to understand your ability to rise."

—Molly Chanson

FOUND THE EMAILS FROM NICOLE WESTON ON THE FOURTH OF JULY.
Interestingly, I found them while on the phone with my friend Sam
just as she was telling me she had found evidence that her husband's
overseas affair never actually ended. Sam had woken up in the middle
of the night, jolted upright with nervous anxiety and beading sweat on
her skin. She checked to make sure Tom was asleep and quietly reached
for his phone on the nightstand. She typed in the password she had
memorized, and the screen magically unfurled. Their texts revealed sex,
bodies connecting, and love.

As Sam relayed her story to me, a squeezing knowing formed in my
stomach that forced me to get off the phone.

"I have to call you back," I interrupted Sam with a sure voice. "I'm
sorry. I'll call you right back."

Hearing Sam talk about her husband's girlfriend, the one she had
suspected, we all had suspected, sent needle-thin pin pricks to the back of
my neck. I asked Sam's husband, Tom, about his girlfriend once, as a favor
to Sam, and when he told me I was crazy, that it would never happen, he
was so believable. So cunning. I felt guilty for even questioning him. What's
wrong with all of us? Why would we mistrust this decent, hardworking man?

Following my therapist Alexa's advice, I tried as best I could to observe
David over the next several days as a witness without expectation. The
problem was that I was so angry it was nearly impossible to enact the
nonjudgmental observer. It was like trying to balance steadily in a yoga
pose and continually yelling at myself when I fell out. The unrealistic
expectation ensured that I would never achieve balance that day.

Sam comes over a few days after the Fourth. She brings a bag of clothes,
necessities, and her small dog, Rex, to stay with us until she has a plan. She

tells me to kick David out. David is working in his home office and comes into the kitchen to say hi when she arrives. I am shocked David can chat with Sam so reasonably with full knowledge of what his friend did to her and what he had done to me. The four of us are best friends, and any betrayal was done to the entire pack. Sam starts out cordial but begins quickly laying into David on my behalf—or maybe our behalf.

"Molly could have died. While you were off cheating with your girlfriend, she could have died."

I revel for a bit as I witness what it is like to have someone fight for me. I hear Sam's supportive words about how hard I'd worked to get sober, how I gave up my career to stay home with the boys, how I needed a partner by my side. Her words sound like they are from another tongue and about another woman. I stand in awe that she can actually be talking about me. I sound good and whole and at least like I've been trying. Through Sam's words and view, I am not a horrible person. I am not unlovable. I am good.

David's friendly demeanor ends at the attack, and he lashes out at Sam. I immediately jump in to save her, and after a few minutes, David and I forget all about Sam and are screaming at each other. Sam grabs our boys to shield them and takes them outside to play.

I want to know what David's girlfriend has that I don't. When did he know he loved her? How did he know? How many times had he told her he loved her? When was their first kiss?

David keeps answering my questions by saying, "I don't know. I don't know." Watching his head shake drives me fucking crazy. How do you fall in love with someone and have no idea how it happens? I want all the details. I need the entire story read to me like a novel so I can understand all the characters and their flaws, their humanity, and their motives. I need to place the truth in my mind about what is wrong with me, why I am not enough, and what I could have done differently. I want to know the reasons this happened so I can make sure I never have to feel this pain again.

The beauty and magic of yoga is that I sit and touch what is real without manipulation or regret. I touch my mat, my skin, my breath. I know the inhale enters through my nostrils, cold at first but then runs warm. I know the air travels fully into my belly and expands it like wind entering a sail. Then, as I continue to take air in, the breath moves further up my torso, where it flares my ribcage and lifts my collar bones. As I exhale, each body part drops and contracts as a result of the breath leaving, first my collar bones, then my rib cage, then belly. This is how the breath moves through my body: it enters through my nostrils, fills my belly, and moves up, then exhales out the same way it travels in. Dirgha pranayama, the three-part breath, calms and sustains me.

In my marriage, I attempted outer perfection in order to sustain. I falsely believed that if I could change—be prettier, sexier, better—I could avoid pain. Yoga teaches me that I might be enough just as I am, humanness and all. Somehow, on my yoga mat, with closed eyes and three-part yogic breath, I trust that there is no one else for me to be.

In the kitchen with David while Sam is outside with the boys, my chest is so tight and hot I think it might combust into red ashes. My jaw squeezes shut and everything out of my mouth is growled between clenched and biting teeth. I am bitterly enraged but afraid to actually scream or move my body. I am afraid I might pick up the glass in front of me and hurl it across the room. I fear that when the glass hits the wall, I might actually break and shatter into a million tiny pieces until there is nothing left but invisible, dangerous shards.

The rage and heat inside me is much more uncomfortable than knowing about the infidelity. I am more ashamed and confused about my anger than about David's actions. I feel out of control in my body and my mind, and I wonder if I have been doing my yoga practice all wrong. How could I call myself mindful? How does a student of yoga find herself in so much rage and turmoil?

Yoga does not promise to take us away from our emotions or to give us a life without problems. Rather, yoga promises that if we do not turn away, if we continually return to ourselves and go in and in, we will discover the power to skillfully navigate emotions, circumstances, and life's challenges, all while staying true to who we are. Much of our pain comes from our own refusal of self. Pratyahara is a practice in not turning away from what is real inside us. Pratyahara is a practice in eliminating outside sensations and distractions so we can actually attend to what is needed right now. We allow what's necessary to flow, even when it's not pretty, rather than shut it all down.

I look at David, his presence wrapping around me and squeezing like a winter gale. My sympathetic nervous system ramps up, senses danger, and even though I am physically safe, the stress puts my cells into fight or flight. My body wants to run, scream, shake, and rage. But I have no idea how to do these things. I know how to meditate and be still. I know how to fold over into child's pose on my mat and allow warm breath to expand into my belly. I know how to close my eyes and rock my forehead back and forth on my mat in order to escape the outside world. I know how to run. But what about now? I don't know how to get away from the vice of nonacceptance, or the heavy, hot anger that jumps and burns like flames around my tender heart. A voice keeps asking: *Is this who I am? Is this my life? Did I ask for this?*

I try to rip David apart with my words, but it isn't working. Even the lowest blows bring no satisfaction. He stands at the counter and takes it, and his silence makes me even angrier. I race upstairs and mutter something about his work suits hanging in his closet.

He chases after me, but not in time. I tear all the jackets and stylish, patterned dress shirts off hangers and throw them into a wrinkled pile on our bed. I sob and snot into every single shirt collar and unbuttoned cuff. I wail about his precious work trips and my bitter loneliness, my worthlessness, and my lack of support. My dramatic scene in his closet is working. David is fuming now, and I have what I need: his attention.

"You better pick all this up." His words add fuel.

"YOU pick it up if you care so much! I don't care what happens to any of these clothes. I don't care about your fucking job and I never did!" I keep adding to the pile.

David turns to walk away, and I run to block him off in the hallway. I throw my entire body up against his, and we collectively slam into the wedding photo that hangs proudly on the wall.

I make a fist, but my nails dig sharply into the soft skin of my palm, so I open them slightly. I tighten my fingers in again, like squeezing a ball. I continue curling my fingers and releasing them as I tempt myself with what to do.

"Punch me in the face. Do it," David taunts me. He never looks away from my eyes.

I close my fingers inward again and swing at his shoulder, but the impact hurts my knuckles, and something inside me cracks wide open, like a hammer dropping on glass. I watch the frame holding the cloudy yet picturesque photo slide sideways off the wall and land face down on the soft hall carpet. I remove my body from David's and run the other direction, down the hallway, down the stairs, and out the front door.

Bright sunshine catches inside my watery eyes, and I want to disappear again. But it is hard in broad daylight. I want to sneak away in the night, alone, and without anyone knowing. I want to breathe in child's pose with my forehead on the ground, in my secret triangle of breath and darkness, unable to see what everyone else in class is doing, and silently hiding the tears that wet my mat.

Bennett and Andrew are climbing the tree in front of our house as Sam urges them on. She catches my eyes, and we hold our gaze. The dust and wind in my chest is garbled now. More than air that flows freely, I have physical particles that bump into one another and cause a scratchy, earthy disturbance in my throat. My chest is like rocks that crunch together as I inhale and wheeze. I don't want to break. I don't want to become invisible. I don't want to be dangerous and jagged. The boys make their way down from the top of the tree, and Sam lifts them gently off the bottom branches.

The boys run toward me. "Mommy, we want a snack! Can we eat it in the tree house?"

I return to the kitchen. The knife in my hand as I slice through apples and cheese feels blunt and off-balance, more like a mallet. The ripping of the plastic bag as I unwrap crackers and lay them on two small plates sounds like stepping on shattered glass. David comes downstairs and stands in front of me, his arms folded, and says nothing.

I am used to this. David stands silently in the doorway when I tuck the boys in at night, leans over my shoulder while I type on my computer, and tries to hold a conversation with me while I take a shower. He doesn't physically touch me, but I feel him all over me, and I can't breathe.

I walk the two plates of food outside to the boys, and when I come back in, David is crying on the floor of Andrew's bedroom.

"What have I done? Look what I did. I'm so sorry. I'll never forgive myself." His fingers claw at the top of his forehead as he cradles his cheeks in his palms. His words come out on inhaled gasps instead of normal exhales, so they jump and skip as he tries to get them out.

My heart leaps at his pain, and I move to console him. The beating muscle in my chest leaks out a tender, caressing ache like someone's warm hand on your bare shoulder, and I want to drop everything, fall on top of him, and tell him it's all OK. Not to worry. I'll fix everything, and we will be OK. This is what happens after all our fights: I apologize; I promise to change; I promise not to make him mad anymore.

This time I stop myself. I recognize my ability to be so easily lured back in, and I am curious how often I have done this, sacrificed myself in order to avoid the conflict and prevent him from feeling any remorse. How often have I taken on all the pain myself so I could protect someone else from feeling this way?

Instead of moving to hug David, I turn the other way. I walk back to his closet and pick up the gray pair of pants flung and wrinkled at the top of the heap. One by one, I rehang each suit, each tie, each button-down shirt, until it's as if no one had ever touched anything.

David's closet is all back in order, and I cry myself to sleep. There is still Nicole, the woman who loves David and who David loves back. What am I supposed to do about that? Sometimes the voice in my head tells me everything will be OK, that I can stay with a man who loves someone else because he probably loves me too, just differently. And we have kids, so I am also obligated to them. Part of being a mom means sacrifice, but at what point are the kids better off because their mom is happy? David said he loves me, but he also loves Nicole.

Then the voice in my head gets loud and emphatic. It tells me I have no choice but to leave. OF COURSE YOU LEAVE YOUR HUSBAND WHEN HE'S IN LOVE WITH SOMEONE ELSE. Why is this circumstance that I thought would be fairly straightforward so confusing and muddy?

My circumstance is confusing because I feel responsible; I feel I deserved it. Like a victim of assault—if I hadn't gone to the party, if I hadn't worn that dress, if I hadn't been so engaging...if I hadn't quit my job, if I'd made more money, if I wasn't so tired, if I wasn't an alcoholic...the affair never would have happened. It is all my fault.

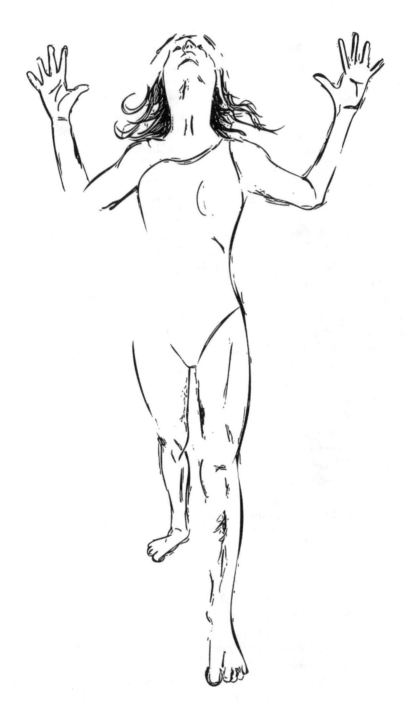

ANAHATASANA : HEART OPENER POSE

PART VI

Dharana : Focus

SINGLE-POINTED FOCUS : CONCENTRATION ON THE BREATH, A VISUAL, OR A MANTRA

"This very practice itself is called concentration: the mind running, your bringing it back; its running, your bringing it back. You are taming a monkey. Once it's tamed, it will just listen to you. You will be able to say, 'Okay, sit there quietly.' And it will. At that point you are meditating. Until then you are training yourself to meditate. Training your mind to meditate is what is called dharana."

—Sri Swami Satchidananda

Dharana is not meditation, not yet. **We practice dharana by bringing our focus to a single sensation, an anchor, or a pain point.** Then, when we get to meditation, we are open, free from distraction and illusions, and able to wholly listen. Dharana removes the blinders of low self-worth and inadequacy so we can settle in and see more clearly who we actually are.

Modern human beings are consummate multitaskers, and that applies to our emotional state as well as everyday tasks. We have mastered how to perceive multiple scenarios at one time and give each stimulus a name, a label, and a pecking order. Humans quickly and skillfully determine what information can be disregarded and what requires our direct focus. We consume and disperse millions of sensory perceptions every second, so the process is instinctual and automatic. We are not even aware we are doing it.

For example, when we walk into a room, we eliminate unnecessary data and tighten our gaze on what matters. Because we all have different pasts and different experiences, what we focus on is different for every person who walks into that same room. Our eyes travel to an object or a scene and fixate on a story and a perception based on our beliefs and conditioning. Beliefs about ourself and beliefs about the world attach to each of our senses and reinforce what we already accept as truth. Dharana gives us an opportunity to question these beliefs and perceptions. Dharana asks us to bring our conditioned world into tight focus in order to explore the possibility that our perceptions may be false; meaning, the stories we continually tell ourselves may or may not be true.

SEVENTEEN

My Drishti

"Our rational minds can never understand what
has happened, but our hearts, if we can keep them
open to God, will find their own intuitive way."

—Ram Dass

ANAHATASANA

SHOCK ERUPTS LIKE A SMALL STONE HITTING GLASS AFTER I FIND
Nicole's emails to David. I drive on the highway, music loud, fiddling
with the heat dial while glancing down at my phone. A small, seemingly
insignificant rock swept up by the driver's tire in front of me, lifts off
the pavement and shoots straight back. The tiny but fast-moving stone
nicks my windshield and startles me with a heavy ping. A small star
forms in the glass, and jagged lines spread out from the center. I stare at
the damage, about the size of my thumb, directly in front of my eyesight.

Nicole, my husband's girlfriend and the woman he loves, is beautiful.
I looked her up online and scrolled through her Facebook account. Her
long silky hair curls buoyantly in each photo, looping around her shoulders
and down across her breasts, which are much larger than mine. I stop
for several minutes on a photo of her seated on a green lawn with two
adorable children who share her heart-shaped lips. Her husband hangs
his arm around her shoulder and leans in close. I deduce from his tender
smile and childlike, blush-colored cheeks that he also loves her. I study his
eyes and examine whether or not he knows, and whether or not I should
tell him.

My mind processes Nicole's existence and what she means to my
husband. The most painful part is wondering what my husband means
to her. Nicole's words, and the fact that she loves David so wholly and
desperately, make me ashamed, like I am unworthy of love. I don't love
my own husband with as much depth and longing as this woman's words
describe; I have never told David I "need" him. I have never asked to

run away with him as if we are the only two people in the world. Maybe we were like this before having kids, but since becoming a mom, my attention and my gaze has traveled more to the babies. I always thought that when the boys were older, David and I could return to one another, to an existence not pulled by small voices and essential needs. But maybe I have slipped away too far. Maybe I am not the same woman I was before having kids, and maybe I won't ever go back. I wrestle with whether or not I could fling myself at David and make all of this go away. What type of woman should I be? What type of woman does he want?

Like I have done my entire life, I try to figure out who the world wants me to be. I focus on fitting in and molding my inner and outer self for the sake of others' satisfaction. I have never considered that the question I should be asking is not *Who should I be in order to deserve his love?* Instead, I should be asking *Who am I? And who will love me just as I am?*

I sleep with a heart-shaped rose quartz stone since finding out about my husband's love affair. The stone gives me something to help stop the spreading pain and the continual blows. I place the cold, heavy stone inside my palm, turn back the covers, and sleep with it squeezed inside my fist. I often wake with the stone still tightly lodged there, afraid to let go and lose it in the sheets. Unlike a sleeping pill to help me forget, the stone offers comfort in the form of a tangible focus, offering solace and hope as I lie in the vastness of the empty bed.

Waking up with the pale pink stone inside my palm is like reliving the truth all over again. The smooth cold surface rubs heavily on my skin, and my fingers ache from my tight grip. Opening my eyes and seeing the rose quartz is like rereading Nicole's emails, her words to my husband. I wake jolted and raw. I want to hide inside the bed and fall deep into the mattress where no one can see me or need me.

Sleep is something I never gave any thought to until I became a mom. Before motherhood, I took sleep for granted. Then I had a baby, and sleep became an indulgent cup of coffee with a long-lost friend, a sunset on the last night of vacation, an opportunity to be savored because soon it would be gone. I dreamed of a lazy Sunday morning where I could actually appreciate my bed and my pillow under soft covers as sunlight blared through the windows, wrapped in the knowledge that I was intentionally choosing to stay in bed. New motherhood was waking in the dark in a startled fit because the baby was crying, and the sun wouldn't be up for another two hours.

The sleepless nights I experience after learning of the betrayal remind me of the sleepless nights as a new mom. And once again, I realize I have forgotten to savor the nights that I did have peaceful sleep and the mornings I woke up to sun streaming through the windows.

I purchased the rose quartz a few years before from a street vendor while on vacation with my sister-in-law in Hawaii. The purchase was spontaneous and in-the-moment.

"Rose quartz," the young girl said as I picked up the stone from the table and rolled it over in my hand. The stone was shaped like a heart, with a pointy bottom and a divet at the top of the curve.

"It's for love and intuition." Her youthful eyes sparkled, and I noticed the colorful scarf she had tied around her small chest as a top. I used to dress like that. I envied her and liked her all at the same time. The stone fit perfectly in the palm of my hand. I liked the weight and the pale, transparent surface with white cracks running through it.

The girl smiled and continued, "It will bring you love." Since I was happily married at the time, I was skeptical. I wondered how many lonely women had walked by her clever stand with heart-shaped crystals and tropical tonics sure to cure any loneliness or broken heart. The young girl sold spells for misplaced love and lost identities. I didn't need the rose quartz for love—I was married. But I happily handed the girl cash for the quartz stone anyway.

Since then the stone has been inside a drawer in my bathroom, near half-used jars of eye cream and tonics, unsure of its purpose. After putting the boys to bed, I pace around my king-sized bed and wonder how I will get through this night. I remember the stone. I march into the bathroom, pull open the drawer, and pluck the pink heart from its spot, confident in my prognosis.

I believe in the magic of Hawaii and the crystal's healing properties. I believe the young salesgirl, with her sparkly eyes, wide smile, and dewy, round cheeks. I didn't know I would be a lonely woman in need of this stone, but here I am.

Focused on myself and my circumstance, I am somewhat unaware that I have not thought about having a drink. I dislike all these feelings in my body, but I know alcohol will only cover everything up, not make it disappear. Numbness is tempting, but I have a sense that I need to stay awake and alert for this moment in order to know what to do next. So in this raw, perfect moment, when it would seem justifiable, I don't drink.

By now, I know not to betray my body and my intuition. I know my intuition led me to find the emails. I only found them because I followed my body's signals as they rose up inside my chest and pricked persistently at my neck. So if I betray my body with a drink, if I betray my truth by giving up, then how am I supposed to listen to what my body will tell me next? I'm in too much pain to betray myself now. Physically and mentally, I've gotten stronger, and this feels like the moment to finally fight for myself.

The crack formed from David's betrayal spreads, unable to stop once it started. When I find Nicole's emails, I can't stop reading her loving words to him. I sit on the safety of our blue couch, the same couch I helped David pick out and order from the furniture store once he'd saved enough money. The same couch I sat on with Bennett when we brought him home from the hospital. The same couch, moved around to three different homes.

In less than a second, the reality of the past year and a half unfolds in front of me. I remember David's trips, the times he told me he didn't answer his phone because it had been switched to vibrate. I think of North Carolina, where Nicole lives and where David has just started traveling. At the revelation, I say out loud to myself, *You are so stupid.* Recently, when David told me how great North Carolina is, I thought we might travel there together sometime. More shame rises as I remember sitting in front of my computer and excitedly clicking through bed and breakfasts for me and David. I painstakingly tried to find us the perfect one. I even called over to David in his office and showed him some of the photos to ask which house he liked better. My effort was real, but the circumstance was an illusion. The trip would never happen, yet I was allowed to plan an entire vacation. The understanding of my fantasy forces real tears out of my eyes, and I shrink even smaller into the sofa.

I know from Facebook that Nicole lives with her husband and two adorable children. I click on her husband's profile and analyze his expression. Is he innocent? He looks happy with his arm around his wife and son. My stomach turns over as I slowly understand how far I have been duped, how easily I have been tricked. I thought the betrayal would stop spreading, but like any small crack, the damage keeps going. At every painful revelation, the spidery threads grow longer and eventually travel across the whole length of the windshield. The entire pane of glass will have to be replaced.

Over the next few days, I piece together my experiences from the last year and try to match them up with what was actually happening under my nose. My reality has been so disrupted, I am like a patient with amnesia who needs every fact verified. I check the phone bill. David and Nicole spoke while we were on vacation in Florida. I remembered I went to a yoga class that morning to practice yoga on a pier with dolphins. David happily stayed back at the hotel with the boys. But when I cross-check the cell phone records, I see he talked to her at the same time as my yoga class for an entire hour. I thought he was playing catch with our boys on the beach. I even have photos of it.

As I process the affair, many of my core beliefs about myself are brought into question, like my low self-esteem and my inability to trust. I thought I was to blame, but now my focus shifts from what might be wrong with me to what is possible. As soul-crushing as the betrayal is, the truth of the affair somewhat relieves my fear that I am crazy. Some of the weight I have placed on my own shoulders lifts with each truthful new breath.

The practice of dharana can incite a shift in perception, so we turn our gaze away from the ever-traversed samskara in order to see an alternate view. With my new knowledge of the affair, I glimpse that I may not need to mold and perfect myself in order to be worthy of love. I glimpse truth: I am not the sole problem in this marriage. I glimpse a moment of freedom. My false, habitual stories peel off like layers of old skin; the gray, paper-thin cells that still hold an imprint flake off to reveal fresh, pink skin underneath. A new possibility. A new story.

I read and reread Nicole's emails because they give me a single and unmoving focus, like staring at a dhristi for balance in yoga class. The emails, the phone records, and the Facebook photos are my obsession for the next several weeks.

Then, I get up the nerve to email her:

Hi Nicole,
You know who I am. Are you in love with my husband? What were you thinking?
If you could please, please, do one thing for me—tell your husband. He deserves to know the truth. And he will find out, no matter how careful you are. He should not have to go through the pain of finding out on his own, like I did.
Also, if you were me, what would you do?
Molly

Nicole writes me back right away:

Hi Molly,
Yes, I am in love with David. I have been for several years. It just happened. Please don't tell my husband. I feel like you hold my life in your hands, and you could set off the bomb at any moment. You will devastate our entire family, including the lives of my two children, if you tell him.
To answer your question, I would stay in your marriage.
Nicole

I write back a pissed-off email explaining that she did this to herself and her children, and whether or not I decide to tell her husband everything would still be on her; it would always be on her, not me. This was typical behavior from David as well, the gaslighting that I continually bought into. Everything was always pressed onto my shoulders. My anger ramps up with every email I write to Nicole, and I know I will never achieve satisfaction. So I finally delete her email address from my inbox.

I attend yoga a few days later and Tyler tells us we are doing an entire class dedicated to heart opener poses. Great, I think. And I nearly walk straight back out of the room.

Instead, I find a sunny spot on the floor and roll my eyes as I unfold my mat and sit down. Tyler tells us the class might stir up some unfamiliar emotions, but I disregard his words. I think I have been stirred up enough recently. No one knows what I am going through, and I assume everyone else's problems are minor compared to my own. I have removed myself from any human connection and am simply trying to survive. I wake up with the boys and make them breakfast. I smile as David goes into his office to work. I tuck the boys in at night before David goes downstairs, and I crawl into bed with my stone, alone.

We begin in child's pose, which I welcome. My forehead touches the mat and my inhale lengthens as my belly expands. We lift up off the mat onto our knees and raise our arms up overhead. I do the flow several times; I inhale to rise up, and exhale to fold down. I rise to the sky for divine guidance and I bow to my mat for grounding and support.

When I lift my upper body and bring my awareness to my heart's place in my chest, as Tyler suggests, an unfamiliar sensation arises, melancholy mixed with shame. Learning that I have been cheated on for the past year is a monumental moment, ripe with opportunity to feel and grieve. But the insurmountable truth forces me to shut down any sensations, especially around my heart. Like a casualty of PTSD, I systematically close all my energetic nadis, persistently, one by one.

Nadis are channels where energy flows. When an experience is too much to handle or too overwhelming for our senses, we tighten around the emotion instead of allowing it to be part of our experience. We stop the flow of energy, and a knot is formed, called a granthi. Emotions have no choice but to move and release if we sit and acknowledge how something has made us feel. But when nadis close, and granthis form, emotions remain in our body. When a similar situation arises that triggers the same emotion, we tighten that feeling down too, forming another granthi, another knot. Knots accumulate like spiritual plaque in our soul and ensure we will never be free from our past.

Now we are standing. I lift my chest to the sky before falling again into forward fold. I lift up halfway with a flat back, raise my arms to a "T" and bend my elbows back. I inhale my right leg behind me into a high lunge and tilt my chest up. A tingling sensation erupts around my heart when I inhale and reach my sternum further upward. I sink deeper into my bent knee and press my elbows further back and away. Shut it down. You can't cry during yoga class. This doesn't have to break you. Stay strong. I lift my right hamstring in order to straighten my back leg even more.

My legs remain strong and supportive while in this version of virabhadrasana (warrior one). I inhale again, as the teacher cues, and tilt my chest higher toward the sky. The class collectively exhales, and we step our right leg up to meet the left. Then we hang back down into forward fold. We continue to bend our knees and lower our bodies down to the mat until we are breathing again in child's pose.

Tyler tells us to notice how we feel in our bodies, if anything has shifted or changed. I feel nothing in my heart. The tingling, uncomfortable sensation is gone. I feel relief in my lower back and legs. Then I notice tears wetting my mat, and I hope we are not asked to come up again soon. I let the tears arrive and fall. I tell myself I can cry with my head between my arms and no one will see, so I stay.

After several breaths in child's pose, Tyler tells us to prepare for the opposite side. I twist my head left and right to wipe the corners of my eyes on the short sleeves of my t-shirt. We rise up from child's pose and meet together in standing. I lift and extend my left leg back into a high lunge and again lift my heart while opening my chest and pressing my elbows back. My tears blur the yellow and white flags hanging off the balcony of the building across the street, and I tip a little to one side before I shift my hips forward and pull in my abdominals to reestablish balance in the lunge.

Through dharana we direct our focus to a single point, which can be our breath, a comforting phrase, or a drishti. The triangle-shaped flags rise and fall with the summer breeze that floats underneath them. The flags are my dhristi, my focused gazing point I have been using for balance. My mind travels to memory. I wonder who lives in the apartment and who put out the flags. I wonder if the flags mean something or if the tenants recently had a party. I wonder if a couple shares the apartment. I remember my own apartment in Chicago where my roommates and I had parties on the closed-off rooftop after we found a small crawlspace in the ceiling. Something grips at me when I broaden my shoulders, lift my chest, and imagine my heart shining outward. The memory of Chicago tugs and squeezes inside my ribcage like an impatient child yanking on my hand. The sensation is sharp and burning, and a warm thread travels up my chest, into my throat, onto the tops of my cheeks, and eventually pours out of my eyes as tears.

EIGHTEEN

The Roles We Play

"Our first teacher is our own heart."

—Cheyenne Prayer

YOGA MUDRA

THE FIRST TIME I FELT MY HEART BREAK I WAS COMPLETELY UNPREPARED. My mom and I drove on a snowy dark highway, just a few days before Christmas, after she had picked me up from taking my college final exams.

My mom's cell phone rang, which made us both jump in the car. Cell phones were new in 1999, and the sound of a ring while driving was still foreign to our senses. I am used to my mom answering the phone as if something is wrong. But usually the person on the other line relieves her, saying everything is fine, and my mom calms down once she realizes there is no danger, no catastrophe.

Mom flipped open her new cell phone and in a panicked, shrill voice said, "Hello?!" I waited for her usual follow-up: "Oh good, I thought something was wrong." But this time her voice dropped to a solemn tone, and I glanced over at her face and expression. Her eyes wrinkled and her lips went completely straight as if she were being given complicated math problems and needed to remember all the addition in her head.

"OK." She hung up and kept driving, looking straight ahead. I wasn't sure she even remembered I was there. I didn't say anything.

Mom started, "That was Dad. Jacob was in a car accident. He's at the hospital, and that's all I know." My mom's eyes stayed fixed on the snowy highway in front of her. The sun had begun its descent in the sky, but darkness arrived quickly because of the snow. My mom signaled and moved over into the left lane and sped up. I looked out the window and saw that we glided by the exit we would normally take home.

"What?" I answered. She hadn't asked any questions on the phone. I had so many questions. "Is my brother alive? Is he paralyzed? Is he talking? Walking? Does he have all his limbs? Who was he with? Where are they?

What happened???" I whirled through all my questions and wondered at the fact that this actually was an emergency and my mom was behaving so nonchalantly, like someone had just dialed a wrong number.

"Molly, I don't know. We have to drive to the hospital and they'll tell us there. It will take at least an hour. We can pray. Just pray."

My stomach knotted up, and my throat swelled with fear. Imagining all the what-ifs sent chills through my body. Pray. I always rolled my eyes at the idea of prayer being a solution. Prayer wasn't going to take away my immediate need-to-know. Prayer felt too detached and required too much surrender when there was so much at stake. But there was nothing else to do, so I folded my hands in my lap, closed my eyes, and bowed my head on an inhale to prepare. Then I exhaled slowly and repeated in my head, "Please let Jacob be OK. Please. I don't want him to die. I don't want him to be paralyzed. Just let him be OK."

My mom and I didn't speak another word the rest of the car ride. I suppose she was praying too.

By the time we arrived at the hospital to see my brother, the sky had turned to night. The snow stopped and the sun disappeared. The sky remained a deep gray, and the thick cloud cover hid any stars. The hospital street lights glowed hazy yellow like candlelit orbs with halos brimming steam around their edges. My mom and I jumped out of the car and half ran, half walked up to the entrance. At some point during our hurried walk, we stopped and grabbed one another's hands. Then we continued in that way, hand in hand, embraced and also bracing ourselves for what we might find.

An ER nurse led us to a room with a door, and we opened it. My brother lay on a bed, his face unbloodied and unbruised, his head tipped to one side, and his eyes closed. But he picked it up and looked at us when we walked in. He awkwardly lifted his arms, which were tethered to machines; thin tape and colored wires clung to his wrists and hands. His hospital gown beamed a bright white and freshly pressed iron marks still creased the fabric.

My gaze shifted to a plastic bag of clothes on the chair next to the bed. Everything in the bag was deep crimson; denim and white cotton now blotted dark red and reminiscent of mortality. Blood that hadn't even dried dripped like a Halloween costume kit on the inside of the white plastic.

A few hours before, my mom and I were shopping at my favorite college store, Urban Outfitters. I loved when my parents came to pick me up from school because otherwise I couldn't afford to buy anything. My mom and I were late getting on the road because I couldn't decide between a sweater and a dress. My mom ended up buying me both because she wanted to get home before the storm. I walked out of the store with my brown paper bag, triumphant and elated. I would have new clothes to wear when I saw my friends over winter break.

I saw a flannel pattern on one of the shirts inside the bloodied bag and thought how quickly clothes can mean nothing. I had labored over the yellow dress or the red one, and which sweater, since I already had something similar in my closet. And just like that, I could've been in a car accident and all my new clothes would be sitting inside white plastic, the soiled rags they actually are, not a priority, and never to be worn.

My focus stayed for a while longer on the plastic bag, and I thought of my new, crisp paper bag in the trunk of my mom's car with the store receipt still inside.

My gaze shifted back to my brother.

I grabbed Jacob's hand and sat halfway onto the bed, "It's OK. Are you OK?"

My brother's emotional state reminded me of my Grandma's when she was dying—resistant and scared. He yanked his hand away and in a shaky, agitated voice forced out, "I'm fine. Where are the guys?"

My brother referred to his friends who had been with him in the car.

"Are they OK?" My brother looked at me for any sign of withholding on my face, any hint of what happened to them. But I had nothing to offer. I didn't even know who he was with or where they had been going.

"Yes, they're OK," I finally answered because I hated seeing him so concerned and fragile. He looked so small inside a hospital gown and behind metal bed railings. My younger brother, the baby of the family, wasn't smaller than me for long. Until he turned five, I could still beat him at arm wrestling. After that, he'd always been stronger. He was also more logical, less emotional, more confident, and ready to take on the world. And likable—my brother was appropriately the most popular kid in school. Unlike me and my sister, who tried so desperately to fit in, popularity was the intended and natural role for our brother. He genuinely liked people. He found something in common with everyone from smokers, to jocks, to teachers. He treated them all with equal love and kindness. People and life were attracted to my brother, a perfect size, a perfect fit.

The year Jacob was voted prom king, my sister Anne and I made him put on the red and white crown he got for winning as if being elected Prom King was a major award. It was like having a celebrity in the family and being popular by association.

My sister Anne and I resisted so many aspects of high school—cliques, trends, homework, sports, rules, and popularity contests. They were all on our list of things that were fake and annoying about growing up in a small town. But we handled our resistance in completely opposite ways. I learned from a young age how to get people to like me and that was to play the part in order to fit in. Like a trained actress, I did my homework, arrived on time, dressed in sparkly school spirit colors on pep rally days. If I behaved perfectly, then no one would have anything to criticize, and I wouldn't get hurt. I acted within the role that had been given to me during childhood: the perfect child, the princess, the adorable little girl in ruffled skirts who sat on your lap and let you hug her.

I knew no one really knew anything about me because I didn't know myself. I donned so many masks and outfits, I gave up the opportunity to get to know myself.

My sister Anne was the traditional middle child who had nowhere to really fit in. She acted as if she didn't care what other people wanted or expected. Anne wore baggy clothes and dyed her hair wild colors to prove she didn't care. She learned to bristle and shut down when people stared or talked behind her back. In junior high, when we moved to a new school, Anne got bullied pretty badly, and I think that she finally decided: *Fuck it. I don't need people to like me. I don't need to fit in. It's way too painful.*

Growing up, Anne refused to leave the house in the appropriate dresses and bows my mom wanted us to wear to church, family parties, and holidays. I shook my head at the tiring fights Anne caused every Sunday. I hated my sister for not just playing along. Nothing was going to change anyway, so why cause such a disturbance?

But Anne fought it every single time. She showed up to family functions disheveled and with a crooked pink bow, blonde hair flying, all because she had to be dragged into the car as she screamed and chastised her outfit. At least I wore my church dress with a prideful smile and hid my resentment underneath my skirt and crossed legs.

I always wondered how my sister and I could be thirteen months apart in age, have the same parents and the same family experiences, yet be so completely and wildly different from each other. As the older sister, I wanted to protect Anne from people's disapproval. I wanted to make her more like me. *Just play along, Anne, and you won't get hurt. It's not that bad.* On the other hand, I admired Anne's grit and conviction so much that I secretly wanted to be like her. I envied her role. Mine felt exhausting and restricted.

But my sister did care. She cared a lot. Bullies and mean comments stung and tormented her heart and her skin. Boiling fire erupted like hives on her tongue and spewed out as toughness but, in reality, hid heartache and a longing for acceptance. She felt she didn't exist, which is probably why she made so much noise.

Anne hung out with her best friend, Lucas. They smoked and drank and skipped school. They had sleepovers, even though Lucas was a boy, and for some reason everyone let them do whatever they wanted. I wasn't allowed to have a boy in my room or be alone in a house with a boy; I certainly wasn't allowed to shut the door. It was clear to everyone that Anne and Lucas had a fated connection. God energy filled the room when they were together, so no one dared touch it.

Lucas died in the car accident that night along with another friend who sat in the front seat. My brother had been sitting in the back, and the police found him wandering around in a snow-covered field after the ambulances arrived. No one had any idea how he even got out of the car. After sliding completely under the trailer of a semi-truck parked illegally sideways on the black, icy road, the boys' SUV was crumpled in half, as if by a machine at a junk car lot.

When the nurse told us Lucas, the driver, had been killed, I excused myself from the hospital room to use the bathroom. My knees shook as I walked on soft, off-white linoleum down the long hallway, afraid I wouldn't make it in time. I shouldn't be sad. My brother is alive. My prayer in the car was answered.

Lucas died.

What is my sister going to do?

Rising panic swelled inside my heart alongside the tears behind my eyes. My chest clawed for a breath I wouldn't allow until I got behind the closed door. I found the bathroom and exhaled an audible scream. Tears streamed down my face as I hit my knees and slid my hands down the side of the cold, tiled wall. I gulped for air, but my lungs contracted as if under water. I removed my hands from the wall, gripped the edge of the toilet seat, and threw up.

My sister had just lost her soulmate. And she's only seventeen. What's she supposed to do now? That crack never goes away. The windshield never gets replaced. You only get one soulmate.

I arrive on my knees on my mat and sit back on my heels. Our teacher trainers at Kripalu are walking us through yoga mudra, the symbol of yoga. I stretch my arms straight out in front of me and clasp my thumbs. I pull my thumbs apart and press my arms forward, which moves my shoulder blades apart and stretches my upper back. I inhale, reach my arms behind me, and interlace all ten fingers into a fist near my lower back. I lift my chest, my heart, and slowly, as I exhale, fold forward over my thighs. I continue exhaling and folding until my stomach rests on my quadriceps and my forehead touches my mat. I reach my fists upward, until my body takes the shape of a small triangle, my hands the peak, and my head and feet each corner.

To come up, the instructors remind us to lead with our hearts. I inhale and use my hands to reach myself back before straight up. I lift my chin and then collar bones. I lift my heart off my thighs. With my eyes closed, I imagine my chest spreading open, as if in surgery, and my heart shines forward, radiating light and love as it guides my entire torso up and off my lap. Twenty years after the life-altering car accident, my heart still fears the pain and grief of life. At first, my chest squeezes in resistance. But as I sit, my heart's rhythm slows down. The beats become regular. My breaths become longer. My brain loosens its grip and calms down. Grief is OK. My pain is valid. And when I allow the tenderness, instead of holding it all in or denying that this pain is for me, the panic goes away.

Since the prom king had just been in a horrific accident and two of our small community's close friends had been killed, we arrived home to a driveway full of cars and a living room full of people. Everyone worried about my brother. Neighbors and friends spoke about trauma, PTSD, and survivor guilt. The prom king must have a purpose, but what is it? My brother didn't have a broken bone or a scratch or even a concussion. To this day no one knows how he got out of the car. The title prom king doesn't come without strings. Neither does the responsibility of being the sole survivor. My brother may have walked away with his physical body unscathed, but the scars on his emotional body, the imprint on his soul created a subtle yet much more complex impact.

My sister walked in the door at the same time my brother finally went to bed. When my mom called to give her the news, she immediately got a friend to drive her home from Milwaukee, where she was in school. I looked at her, and she looked at the Christmas tree in the other room, all lit up and glittering. I could tell she had been crying the entire car ride home. She asked me about Jacob. *Yes, he's fine. How are you?*

But her gaze was gone. She was already running into the other room to hug some of our friends who came by. They were speculating about how Jacob survived. They talked about heaven and the possibility of angels. Anne immediately turned and went into her bedroom. She couldn't take it. She couldn't take the heartache of losing her friend, her love, and having no one who understood. She couldn't take the conflicted welling up of losing Lucas and having her brother here alive.

When our emotions don't fit into a form, and we can't quite play the role we know so inherently, we experience inner turmoil and possibly guilt. When we feel both gratitude and grief or maybe think we should feel an experience differently, we bury rather than allow the true and shameful parts to rise to the surface. Parts of my sister shut down that night. Nadis closed, forming tightly bound scars, and a light went out that I've never seen return.

A focused gazing point, a drishti, also means a point for concentrated intention. We can choose to close off the nadi and live in illusion and denial, or we can choose to open ourselves to pain and truth, even when the truth is that our heart has been ripped open and we don't know when it will heal. As much as we rely on our brain to process all the information thrown at us in a given second or day, it's not capable of understanding our full experience. Our brain is not always accurate. Often, we need to rely on our heart and our body to present us with emotions that need to be released.

Until there was Nicole, I never knew I could actually feel my heart. Especially at night, when I turned down my covers and climbed into bed exhausted, the deep pain in my chest surprised me, and I couldn't sleep. Sleeping with a rose quartz stone inside my hand focused my attention on something solid, weighted, and tangible. Rolling the stone over, squeezing it, and examining the sensation in my palm allowed me to touch something that represented love and openness. The heart-shaped stone became my access to the present moment, and even though I slept and woke in pain, the physical stone helped quiet the narrative story of what David's betrayal meant for me and for my understanding of love. The quartz was my drishti, my touchpoint to my emotions, and my reminder to keep my heart open, despite it being broken.

I went in for a routine physical exam in college when the nurse discovered what she thought was a heart murmur. After an echocardiogram and stress test, doctors discovered I had mitral valve prolapse, which is how my grandfather died. My mom, aunts, and uncle all have MVP too. My mom and my aunt both had open heart surgery in order to repair their valves, which grew weaker and weaker with lifestyle and age. The more stress on your heart, from heavy lifting, unhealthy eating, or carrying children, the more the valve leaks, and the damage spreads like an untended crack in the windshield.

When I had the echocardiogram done in college, I sat upright on the hospital bed, hooked up with suction cups and wires, and watched a screen. Green and red lines moved rhythmically up and down on the monitor and demonstrated my regular heartbeat. Then the doctor pointed to the small extra line that shouldn't be there, the part that indicated a backwash of blood and a weak heart valve. I was fascinated and felt slightly special. Only 2 percent of people get this heart condition and I had it. The extra line on the monitor made me feel interesting, at least to the doctor who focused on my condition.

Feeling my broken heart during a yoga pose is different than feeling my heart medically. Lifting and stretching my heart upward feels risky, as if I am a tree growing sideways over a cliff, and the further I reach my branches toward the sun, the harder my roots have to work to keep me attached to land. My damaged heart valve has been there inside my chest my entire life, and I've never noticed a thing. It took doctors twenty years to discover the leak, and from the outside, no one would know I was walking around with an irregular heartbeat from a valve that functions basically fine, except for the tiniest, slightly off rhythm.

The exposure on my heart of my husband being in love with another woman makes me wonder if the damage to my soul is also unrepairable.

Walking the world with an open, broken heart might be admitting a weakness, or maybe it's a discovery that our human heart was never meant to stay intact. So our intention, our drishti, is not to protect and avoid pain, but to continue stretching and reaching our branches toward love, even with knowledge that we will break and fall.

After David's betrayal is revealed, I keep going to yoga classes. But I am petrified of every heart opener pose because I know they will make me cry. I've held this sadness in for so long, long before I was married, or had children, or found out about Nicole. My belief: *If I am happy, others are happy. And once I allow the tears to start dropping, I don't know if I'll ever get them to stop.*

NINETEEN

Glimpsing the Soul

"Each moment holds the entire Universe of who you are
and every second is a supernova waiting to happen."

—Nausicaa Twila

FALLEN STAR POSE

I LEFT MY OFFICE A FEW MINUTES EARLY IN ORDER TO MAKE COPIES before teaching my 9 a.m. class at Columbia College Chicago. I checked my phone as I walked down the hall to see any updates in the group text about our friend Leane. Leane had undergone heart surgery a few days before, and her husband, Will, promised to let us know how she was doing. The text Will sent right after surgery said everything went perfectly, that he was heading home to be with their ten-month-old daughter, Eleanor, and Leane would be resting through the night.

The updates suddenly turned tragic when he alerted us he had received a phone call from the hospital shortly after returning home. Leane was not coming off the anesthesia within the normal timeframe. Will's next email detailed the blood clot that had ruptured in Leane's brain and the necessity of a medically induced coma to control any swelling and consequent brain damage from the bleeding. Two days later we were still waiting for the email that told us Leane was fine and waking up.

Walking to the copy room, I saw a new text from our friend Meg: "Oh my God! check your email."

The already dim hallway felt small and over-crowded as I prepared myself for news I didn't want to hear. Like when my phone rang four times in a row in the middle of the night, and I knew before answering it someone had died; it was my grandma. Then, a few years later, my uncle.

I slowly scrolled my finger over to the email on my phone. Still walking, the narrow hallway parted and I arrived in the open foyer. Sunlight streamed through newly added windows on the eighth floor, and students made use of the communal study area where low tables and chairs sat on top of colorful, patterned carpet.

The email was from Leane's husband, Will—a final update. "It looks like I'm going to have to let my baby go."

I stopped abruptly near the copy room. Leane had been in a coma for two days. I'd said prayers every night and every morning, and knew in my heart she would be OK. She would see her miraculous daughter, Eleanor, and raise her. I would see Leane again and finally make time for her to visit me in Wisconsin.

I continued reading: "Leane will be taken off the breathing tube...tomorrow morning...if you want to say goodbye...you are welcome...but come soon...we are at Northwestern Memorial...room 1412."

I looked up at the bright circular ball that hangs high in the sky and wondered at its capacity to leak massive sunlight through the atrium windows and onto all the surfaces inside this building—the carpet, the tables, the people. Students and instructors rushed past me, and my hands began to shake. I stood at the edge of the hallway inside a beam of sunshine that streamed uniformly across the tops of my slip-on shoes. I didn't bother to move out of anyone's way. When my knees regained consciousness, I turned around and started walking back to my office. I quickly grabbed my coat and bag, then turned again to reach for a sheet of paper from the printer on which to write a note.

Stay. Stay in the pose, the instructor reminds us. I hold plank on a summer Saturday morning a few weeks after finding out about David's affair. Today we are practicing yoga on the beach. The lake echoes her familiar sounds. Waves lap rhythmically against white piers as metal fishing boats glide lazily by, dragging nearly invisible lines through the water's surface that hold tempting, stinging treats. My stomach has been in knots for days, so holding plank and the rippling tightness in my abdomen feels like redemption. Maybe if I allow the flames to consume me, like a controlled, necessary brush fire, the pain will be extinguished more quickly. My abdominal muscles wiggle and shake like the water that reflects the morning sun. I tilt my head in order to avoid a sun ray aimed straight at my eyes, and I intentionally cinch my abdominals inward, igniting them, and silencing their pleas for relief. The muscles tighten around my back and sides, and even down my buttocks and legs. I exhale warm breath, which mingles with the cool lake air, and I command myself to remain perfectly strong and still for as long as it takes.

Leane always looked out for me. We met in an elevator on the first day of graduate school, and she immediately wanted to know all my professors. I thought it was an odd, somewhat nosy question, but I pulled out my printed schedule from my backpack and read all the last names to her anyway. She responded quickly to each name with interesting facts about their mannerisms, their homework load, and little tips for successfully completing their course. Somehow, on the forty-five-second elevator ride, she not only gave me much wise advice, but we also became immediate friends. Leane was good at that; she knew exactly what people needed in the moment.

On a subsequent elevator ride between classes, we learned that we both had heart conditions; Leane's, however, was more severe than mine. My doctor discovered my irregular heartbeat in college during a routine checkup. My condition was something to monitor, but was not alarming. I could still go on in life as normal. My weak heart valve may require surgery at some point, but in the meantime, it was nothing to be concerned about if I kept up a healthy lifestyle.

Leane took my diagnosis more seriously and always cautioned me: "Take care of yourself. Protect your heart." Doctors had discovered Leane's heart condition at birth, and she had already undergone two surgeries by the time I met her in graduate school. Because of her heart, she could not have children. If she conceived, her deficient heart would not make it through pregnancy or childbirth, and she would die. Hearing Leane tell me so matter-of-factly in an elevator that at fourteen she had been told she would never be able to have children sent aches and shivers to my own heart space. I held her gaze silently after she told me and waited for her to say more. I tried with my brainwaves to coax out the emotion that must really be on her mind. But she smiled and reassured me, "I've accepted it. If Will and I want to have children, we'll adopt."

Leane also had to refrain from certain exercise, and she most likely would have a shorter life span. Surgeries could prolong her heart's ability to continue working, but she would never be old. This was also stated matter-of-factly but not disingenuously, and I marveled at Leane's ability to be present and at peace with her short life. Maybe the definite time span made presence easier for Leane. Maybe not knowing when you will die, but at least having an estimate, allows you to embrace a more finite window and therefore understand the capacity and integrity of each day, each moment, and each second of life.

I didn't have any of these setbacks; I had my entire life ahead of me to use however I wanted. Gazing at my future was like staring into a dark tunnel with no end and no lamp post in sight. Each day I stepped further into blackness and tried to assemble a working life that might shed some light on my journey. My life plan was to collect and accumulate—a job, a husband, and a family. These would bring me wholeness and a sense of purpose.

"If I could work out, I would." Leane and I did gentle yoga together, since that was approved for her heart. She encouraged me to run more, but I didn't really like exercise, and it was easy to use her as my reason for practicing yoga.

Several years after she is gone, on this sunny Saturday morning, I think of Leane while holding tightly onto plank pose and trying my hardest to fight the accumulating grief that rises inside my core and pricks at the surface of my skin like still-burning ash. The instructor tells us that from plank, we will move into fallen star pose. I shift my energy to my right oblique in order to pick up my right leg from its dug position in the sand. When I lift my leg, my muscles respond. My core stokes the heat in my right side and allows me to smoothly float my leg under my body and over to the left. Naturally, as I straighten my right leg under my left and out to the side, my torso twists upward and my heart opens toward the sun.

By the time I got down to the third floor from my office, time had begun to feel impossibly fast, like every second I wasted Leane was dying, and I would miss her forever. I couldn't stop moving because if I did, something bad would happen. I had to get to Leane before she was gone. I ran to my classroom and found a student sitting on the floor outside the locked door. They all gathered like this prior to the start of class—students and their backpacks crumpled over phones and computers lined the edges of the hallways. They barely looked up when the teacher opened the classroom door.

I approached a shy black-haired girl, my student waiting patiently right outside the door to our classroom. "I need to cancel class. I'm going to the hospital to see a friend. It's an emergency." My voice shook and sounded unlike my assertive, teacher voice. The words were slow and clumsily crawled up my throat as I spoke them out loud. I handed my student the blank printer paper and asked her if she could write a note for the rest of the class. "I forgot a pen. And tape it to the door. I also forgot tape." Wide-eyed and concerned, my student assured me she would take care of it. But my body was already halfway down the hallway.

I rushed past a clump of students waiting for the elevator and opened the door to the stairwell. If presence was standing still, I couldn't right now. I headed out the front door and into the sunny fall air. Students stood everywhere. They smoked cigarettes and were plugged into headphones; their bodies leaned against walls and large city flower pots. Buses groaned as they slowed to pick up passengers and then veered back into traffic. I raised my arm to signal a cab. "Northwestern Hospital," I said as I threw my bag across the seat and climbed in.

When the cab door shut, the muffled hum of the city enveloped me. I finally noticed my own inhale and caught my breath. I couldn't do anything about the Chicago traffic or the cab driver or the lane he chose, so I had no choice but to be. I stared out the window and noticed all the life going on around me. It reminded me of when my boys were born, and I marveled at the world's ability to just exist as if nothing was happening. And that's how life is. You move through your day oblivious to the fact that someone is dying in a hospital bed or home with a new baby and suffering from postpartum depression. When you are the one suffering, your world becomes eerily still, and the rest of society just hums along.

When something grabs our attention, it's because we've offered ourselves a moment of presence. Presence is continually available, not only during tragedy or loss. Our minds and our egos trick us into thinking that we must charge ahead and that time is escaping us every second we stand still or sit down. But sitting still and allowing ourselves to be takes courage and stamina. Like a controlled burn, silence and stillness ignite truth and allow it to rise to the surface of our being like a beckoning smoke signal. What are we avoiding and what do we need to hear? Maybe compassion, maybe forgiveness, maybe a simple acknowledgment that we are in pain.

My boys were born in Northwestern Memorial. Chicago was where I brought both my babies home. We lived on the second floor of a red brick building that was built in the 1880s. When I first walked by the building, I was single and on the hunt for an apartment. I saw the for sale sign, and even though I was searching for a rental, I stopped and looked up. Somehow, I already knew the building was mine. The red bricks and muddy exterior spoke to me as I stepped back on the sidewalk and examined the structure. I admired the charm of the black iron gate and the grit of the dirty peeling overhangs. The third floor came to a peak at the top, typical of this old Chicago style, and slightly mismatched bricks indicated where some had been replaced over the hundred years it had stood in this spot, maintained but not completely restored.

A few months later, after securing rental agreements from tenants and negotiating a deal for the down payment, the traditional Chicago three-flat was mine. The single rectangular window below the peak became the boys' nursery; it sat centered like a bird's nest, safely tucked between branches. When David and I moved out of the building, I left the yellow and white gingham curtains hanging in the nursery window, and the last time I drove by, they still waved at me.

We moved out of Chicago to Wisconsin for a quieter life with the boys, but I still commuted into the city to teach. Only a month before, Leane had joked with me on Facebook, "I hope the commute from Wisconsin isn't killing you!" Leane's sense of humor envied our group of friends. Even though she had a refined and somewhat quiet personality, she could deliver a small jab or crass comment with absolute grace and just the right amount of edge. It was always gently kind and completely hilarious.

I arrived at the hospital, paid the cab driver, and checked Will's email again to see what room she was in. I took the elevator to the fourteenth floor and greeted the staff at the front desk. They pointed to a dimmed, quiet room with the door cracked open. Timidly, I paused, then pushed the door slightly more open with my palm. Leane's room was dark compared to the brightly lit nurses' station, and I was immediately taken hostage by the somber hospital air. Machines whirred and buttons blinked, and Leane lay still on a bed in the center of her crowded room. Will stood up immediately and gestured me all the way in; he gave me a hug and cried a little on my shoulder. "I'm so sorry," I whispered in his ear. I didn't know what else to say.

Another man whom I didn't know sat in a chair under the one window in the room; he introduced himself as Leane's brother from Canada. The window shades stayed drawn more than halfway and blocked much of the afternoon sun. Will extended his arm toward Leane's body and sank back into his chair in the shadowed corner as if to give me privacy.

God, I think, Leane would hate this. She would hate that I am here. She would hate that her sick and dying body is on display for anyone to see. Her bare feet dangled out from under the thin blue blanket, and I moved to cover them, to warm them up, but I stopped when I saw the purple veins like rivers of fish on her swollen white skin. Her hair was a dirty afterthought, matted down and pulled back to allow for the stickers and wires connected all around her. The breathing tube in her mouth made her lips wide and puffy, and distorted her otherwise beautiful face. Her hands had been placed like a soldier by her sides and the blanket neatly pulled and tucked up under her chin. No movement. There was no flow in the room, only distant city traffic outside, fourteen floors below.

I picked up Leane's left hand, soft and weighted, like a baby's body when he finally falls asleep on your chest. I wanted her to know I was there, even if I was too late, and that it was going to be OK. I promised her I wouldn't remember her like this, that she was safe. I closed my eyes and imagined the last time we hugged outside a noisy Chicago café. I breathed in her warmth and breath and sweetness. I wanted her to feel mine, but I felt guilty as I stood here with combed hair and my own air inside my lungs.

"I don't think she's in there." Leane's brother voiced out loud what I already knew from the second I picked up her hand.

He went on, "She was here, and then we felt something change. She's not here anymore." I nodded with a reluctant understanding and was taken aback by how much a world can change in a matter of hours. Just that morning I took another sip of my coffee, shook off sleep, and drove carefully along the dark road to the train, mindful of any deer that may be crossing. Two months into my new, long commute to the city, I drove to catch a 6:25 a.m. train. This is the painful trip Leane had often teased me about. This morning, like all my early drives, the sun hadn't even begun awakening, so even though it was technically day, the sky was pitch black and full of twinkling stars. Coming around a curve, I thought of Leane in the hospital, still not knowing her fate. I thought of her husband, Will, and her daughter, Eleanor. I wondered when she would wake up from her coma. Maybe she'd wake up today. It had been several days, and Leane was resilient, able to accept, and able to graciously move forward through any circumstance or curveball with determination. She must wake up; nothing else made sense.

Because of her heart condition and not being able to carry a baby inside her own body, Leane spent years trying to adopt. Despite her optimism and acceptance of her liability, Leane still cried every time she opened a friend's baby announcement in the mail. We can accept and even move forward, but there always may be grief and pain to let out if we are honest. The baby announcements were a reminder of her own fate and maybe her own existence. Leane fought for her brief spot in the world as long as she could.

When the adoption didn't work out, Leane and Will ended up finding a wonderful surrogate mother, an option they had not originally considered. Despite doctors telling her she would never be able to have children, Leane went ahead and had her own daughter.

I laughed when I thought about it. Eleanor was about to turn one, so Leane dying didn't seem to be the logical course of the universe.

Tears hit my eyes while driving. I felt Leane laughing with me. Why did I get up this early in the morning in order to take a train from Wisconsin to Chicago to teach a class? Why was I leaving my babies for this job? What was really at stake?

I hoped she would wake up today.

I checked my phone once again for an update from Will. I put my phone back in the console just as I came to another sharp curve in the road and started down the hill toward a slightly more lit town. As I made the turn, my eyesight locked onto an intensely bright star . . . and then, the star fell straight out of the sky.

My insides dropped down. They fell right along with the star and broke knowingly on top of the Earth's horizon.

The star's descent was much different from other shooting stars I had seen. It did not streak triumphantly sideways and quickly disappear. It did not leave a trail of fanfare behind it. This star sat patiently, shining bright, until my eyes made the connection. Then it arched very slightly upward, like a hand waving, before it dropped straight down and disappeared completely into blackness. No streak, no fanfare. No more light. My heart sank right along with the star. Leane just died. She just waved good-bye.

DANDASANA : STAFF POSE

PART VII

Dhyana : Meditation

STILL THE MIND AND DWELL
IN THE SPIRITUAL LIFE

"Here is, in truth, the whole secret of Yoga, the science of
the soul. The active turnings, the strident vibrations, of
selfishness, lust and hate are to be stilled by meditation,
by letting heart and mind dwell in spiritual life, by
lifting up the heart to the strong, silent life above,
which rests in the stillness of eternal love, and needs
no harsh vibration to convince it of true being."

—Sri Swami Satchidananda

Dhyana is the seventh limb of yoga and means "meditation." The literal translation of dhyana in Sanskrit is "absorption" or "union," which Patanjali calls concentration on higher aspects of reality. According to yoga philosophy, dhyana is achieved when we regularly practice the first four limbs and when we combine the fifth and sixth limbs—presence and focus—in order to gain an awareness of true Self. Yogis have called this experience glimpsing the soul, and it feels like a union with oneself, a sense of completeness, with no effort.

Dhyana is when we remain fixed on truth, the object, or the moment, instead of running from story to story in the mind.

TWENTY

Present Heals Past

"We destroy the veil that covers the inner light. Prakasa,
the light within, is covered by a veil of mental darkness.
What is the best way to remove a veil? By pulling the
threads out, one by one, until it exists no more."

—Sri Swami Satchidananda

B Y THE TIME I CHECKED MY EMAILS AND TEXTS THAT MORNING, I HAD hoped the experience was a fluke, that I had somehow made up the synchronicity and that it was merely coincidence. But now I stood next to Leane's body in the hospital. Her brother's comment that she had already gone affirmed the knowing I felt this morning while watching the star fall into darkness. Still holding her hand, I said a prayer. I thanked her for the light she brought into my world, for all she taught me about the precious moments, and I leaned in to kiss her damp forehead. I hugged her body, now empty of her soul, and wondered about her journey. When the star waved at me and disappeared out of the sky, I felt a moment of divine perfection, like everything made sense and everything was connected. Time stopped and I glimpsed transcendence.

Experiences like this are part of the fifth and sixth limbs of yoga—presence and focus. We feel moments of perfection and wholeness, witnessing our true self when we are faced with something so imminent, finite, and focused that we cannot help but understand our oneness. We witness a birth or the transition from life to death, and these acute moments bring us so close to presence that we actually zero in on the moment, undistracted by thoughts, stories, or ego.

My gratitude for this moment, the experience Leane shared with me during her death, was like witnessing God. I knew something beyond me existed, and I only needed to remember that star falling to connect back to who we are.

In fallen star pose, the instructor suggests we lift up through our side and raise our left arm high in order to find space and strength in the balance. I want to hold myself through the pain of my husband's betrayal, but I also want it to pass quickly. It's only been fourteen days since finding out, and I'm not sure I can handle any more fire in my body. I consider giving up and pushing back into downward facing dog in order to exhale fully out of my open mouth and give my core some relief. As I imagine moving into a resting pose, my shoulders automatically loosen and release down my back. My neck extends and the weight of my head lightens. I am unsure if I have the strength to stay. I check in with my muscles. I loosen the grip in my upper thighs and shift everything into my right oblique, breathing through the fatigue. I think again about Leane and her determination, her grace, her ability to remain present despite circumstance. I rise out of my right side and extend my left arm up and behind me. I reach upward to balance the weight. I stay. I honor the pain. If my body falls from exhaustion, soft sand will catch me, and I will be safe.

With my arm extended upward, my abdominals no longer ache like they did while in plank or before the full extension of the pose. My body extends through five points: a foot and hand in the sand, a foot and hand pointing out and back in opposite directions, and my crown aiming directly at the sun. The pain in my abdominals shifts as my limbs engage and work to disperse the weight.

Focused presence is the acknowledgment that time is manmade, a form we created in order to function. Despite time's necessity to society, the focus on time brings us further from our divinity. Maybe everything is happening all at once, like time is forever but also instant. This is why I feel the pain of Leane's death at the same time I feel the pain of David's affair. Even though the events happened many years apart, through yoga, I experience the pain of each moment as if they are simultaneous. Like the muscles I use to transition through poses, the same space gets squeezed, the same place in my heart aches, and the same energy begs to be acknowledged and released. Nadis are opening that I had closed a long time ago. Past pain and heartbreak that never got healed reemerge. Emotions that were never allowed to flow seep out through bursting pipes. Blocking off the sensations of a painful experience only makes the energy dormant for a while, until something else comes along to open it back up. Our tendency to avoid or ignore these emotions is a way of not trusting the moment and not trusting ourself. Emotions flow, which means they change. If we have the courage to feel and allow for the flow, we will notice the changing energy; we will notice that the pain is not as scary as we thought, and it will always move. I promise, your pain will move.

The next morning I was dropping the boys off at preschool when I got the text from Will announcing the official date and time of Leane's death. I heard my phone ding and already knew what it said, so I continued to help Bennett find his slippers in the bin on the floor. My friend Jen was dropping her son off as well and handed my other son, Andrew, the matching slipper to his Spiderman pair. Our three boys ran into the classroom and we both stood up and waved them all goodbye for the morning.

"I have some good news," Jen said as we started walking down the hall and I pulled out my phone. She knew about Leane, that I visited her yesterday, and that she would die.

"I'm pregnant." I looked away from my phone and turned toward Jen. She smiled. My body lightened with joy for my friend. I knew how long they had tried. I hugged Jen and told her how happy I was. For some reason, I said "thank you" because her news relieved some of the burden from me and shifted my pain, just for a moment.

When we move into fallen star pose on the other side, I carefully lower my extended left arm and pull my right leg back under my body; I roll mindfully back into plank, back into my core, ready to rotate my body in the other direction, intentional about not letting go, not now. My obliques burn from the pose. One more lifted extension, one more side, and I know I am done. In plank, my body visibly shakes, and I consider Leane's fall out of the sky. She went from shining to dark in one second, and then, maybe in a world I cannot see, she arrived at shining again? Is that how death is? Is the transition slow and also immediate? Was her coma an opportunity for me to say goodbye, even though she had already said goodbye in the sky many hours before I arrived next to her body in the hospital? Is anything actually chronological?

Still in transition, I prepare myself to lift up one more time into fallen star pose. I bend my left knee up and in, and extend it gently out and under my right, planted leg. I float my right arm high above my head and slightly back, and extend my fingers upward to carry some of the weight. I imagine my entire body as a star, reaching and shining in all five directions. Sunlight bounces off the water, gets caught in my eyes, and Nicole's love for my husband creeps into my mind.

Her letter stated the words, "I love you." Reading someone else say I love you to your spouse is the strangest experience; it's as if presence has collapsed, and what you thought was real never actually existed. Nicole and David didn't consider me at all. I feel the intense pain of betrayal and realize I am gripping my right toes fiercely into the sand as if I don't trust the rest of my body to hold me up. Tears arrive and fall, and I replay the nights of guilt and shame. I wilt like soft petals underneath hot sun, and my body drifts into memories of the times I went to bed convinced that everything was my fault, the times I begged my husband to tell me if there was someone else, and the times I knew in my heart what was real but refused to rely on my own intuition.

I turn my body away from the sunlight and sink my lifted hand into warm sand. I lay on my stomach and close my eyes, hoping to disappear as the rest of the class continues. It's not really the affair that causes me such conflict, it's the feeling of not existing and of not trusting myself. I remember that girl, I remember Leane, and I want to fade away. Like a fallen star, I want to drop right out of the sky.

ATMAN

I took dance as a little girl because I loved music and I loved dancing. But I hated the stage and people watching. I felt evaluated, like the audience was grading me on whether or not I had learned and perfected all the moves. I never enjoyed the recitals because I focused on the audience's approval and the thick, uncomfortable makeup on my face and whether or not it was smudging. How did they see me, and was I doing it right? So caught up in the effort to not screw up, I appeared clunky and unnatural on stage. I wasn't dancing as myself, like I might dance in my bedroom when no one is watching. I danced on stage as a performer, during which I saw myself as separate. I craved the applause in order to justify my existence, and I was willing to morph myself into whatever shape they expected of me.

I started my meditation practice five years ago. I was married with young toddlers, and my day-to-day life was chaotic. I thought meditating would calm me down. I forced myself awake in the morning at 5 a.m. before my boys woke up and lit a candle in my office. I sat in a fluffy chair I had purchased at a thrift store and covered in an old faux fur rug. I crossed my legs and tucked my ankles gently under my thighs. I opened my palms on top of my knees and closed my eyes. I had no idea what I was doing, but I set a timer for eleven minutes and tried not to open my eyes again until the vibrating gong sounded.

Sometimes I went in with an intention, like to feel compassion or to send love and healing out to someone else. I sat and stared at the blackness behind my eyes and waited for any sensations, any clues that the meditation was working. Often, some clarity came. I knew what to do next, or I sensed an overall emotion of peace and ease, like I was exactly where I was meant to be. Other times I became restless and the minutes dragged along. I'd cheat and peek at the clock on my phone. Meditation changed from day to day and minute to minute. I misunderstood that this is normal, that meditation is not silence but rather absorbing all that we are in that moment. As a perfectionist, I wanted to make sure I was meditating correctly in order to receive the highest benefit, so I googled, read, and wondered if I was missing something. Is this even working? I must be doing it wrong.

But after weeks, months, and years of sitting in silence, I noticed more subtle shifts. Maybe I still went through my day frazzled and stressed. Maybe I still became impatient with my boys. Maybe I still engaged in unhealthy behavior. But my overall ability to hear my intuition and trust my own voice became stronger. My inner voice made more sense. I listened. For the first time, I realized I actually had a heart and a soul who wanted to talk to me and guide me. I sensed my heart was becoming an ally; we were on a path together, and my body appreciated the overdue acknowledgment of my soul.

I indulged every morning in silence in order to find truth and understanding. What I didn't know is that while meditation does bring insight and clarity as well as an ability to trust and know yourself, meditation does not let you dismiss reality. What I thought of as "rising above" was actually an attempt to escape my life and my feelings. But with daily practice, the truth always emerges, and we realize that meditation will not whisk away our problems or make it so we don't care. Actually, meditation may bring more emotion to the surface, parts of ourself we have dismissed and pushed down. I still feel all the stings of life, but meditation has increased my capacity to stay. Like a great pine that does not attempt to thwart its existence on top of the mountain, my branches at times are heavy with wet snow and may even threaten to snap. But I accept the heaviness and the weight. I know I am that pine, so there is nothing else for me to try and be—other than to be here.

Traditionally, meditation may be seen as sitting still, closing our eyes, and trying to get our mind to go blank. But dhyana doesn't always need to be experienced on our mat. I have experienced dhyana while walking briskly down a boardwalk in Miami, headphones turned way up blasting P!nk. Music's vibration shakes out hidden truths that I welcome when they float up to the surface. When I'm driving, walking, observing nature, or listening to music, there have been times I've experienced the calming breezes of Atman, which some describe as God. During these moments, I smile and time stops. Maybe while watching the leaves flutter in the wind on a tall tree, maybe while observing a quiet snowfall outside a church window at midnight, maybe while stepping into a warm shower and feeling the water bead up and run down my skin. During these moments I am one with myself, and nothing else needs my attention.

Meditation is not just about us. Union means we not only acknowledge our own divinity, but everyone else's. Through the practice of meditation, we learn we are not separate at all. There are no roles we need to play to fit in, no choreography we need to learn, and no face we need to paint on. In fact, if not for our individual experiences, we are all the same at our center. What would the world be like if we saw everyone as ourselves? This awareness of our oneness releases an uncomfortable amount of compassion and understanding for every single person on the planet.

Of course, like all the limbs, dhyana is a continual practice; achieving meditation once, understanding our true self once does not guarantee enlightenment forever. This is why we return. We return to our mat and our practice because it is human nature to forget. We return in order to remember who we are and to remember our connection.

We believe that meditation is impossible, or we resist the gift due to the constant barrage of thoughts and stories that enter our mind as a result of being human. Just as we understand our wholeness, the next minute we doubt ourself. Meditation does not actually mean our mind has to empty; meditation means we acknowledge what comes up long enough to notice it change. Like wind that flutters through a tree in full bloom, we create space in the mind between thoughts so we are able to actually listen and discern truth from fear. A meditation practice teaches us not only to allow but also to absorb and feel, so that despite outside circumstance, we actually change.

Meditation has made me a better person. And not because I am perfect all the time, but because I accept my imperfections and my irateness. I am kinder to myself and to others. I own my path and respect the spiritual paths others need to walk. This shift in my perspective has changed my life. When we let go of criticism and judgment, of control and of right and wrong, we see a broken yet beautiful world, and the ache of humanity beats much differently in our hearts than the judgment and blame we held before.

With meditation, my attachment to the material world and all its labels disappears. The words and names for things, and my personal justification of the form, fade away:

Infidelity	Affair	Betrayal
Lies	Marriage	Vows
Commitment	Wedding	Family
Promise	Love	Not enough
Unworthy	Broken	Failure

During meditation, my story shifts subtly into the background of my mind. The veil lifts, and the truth emerges for the first time. None of these words or my perceptions of them have anything to do with me. My expectation of the promise—the promise of marriage, the promise of motherhood, and the promise of true love—have all kept me away from myself. My attachment to a form—of what a relationship should look like—has kept me in a cage. Collecting roles and titles does not bring me closer to Self. Removing roles and titles does not mean I have failed. My circumstance is not personal; it simply exists.

When my ego threatens to pull me away from Atman, from my light and my truth, I can return to meditation to remember who I am. I can sit. I can walk. I can dance. I can sing loudly in the car when no one is listening. I can also cry unashamedly in the car when no one is watching.

TWENTY-ONE

Warrior Woman

"Why, if it was an illusion, not praise the
catastrophe, whatever it was, that destroyed
illusion and put truth in its place?"

—Virginia Woolf

BADDHA VIRABHADRASANA

A SLIVER OF THE OCEAN IS VISIBLE BETWEEN TWO HIGH-RISE BUILDINGS on the windy Miami rooftop. A carefully rolled up white towel and complimentary bottle of water sit at the front right corner of my yellow yoga mat, which matches the hotel's branded color scheme. Deep blue water meets sky and the two look like one, a vast blue wall that has no beginning or end. With such an infinite sky, I wonder if I am even on the planet. Or is this a movie set, and I would crash into solid mass if I sailed far enough toward the horizon.

A month after finding the emails, I tried to get hold of myself, so I got on an airplane to Miami in the heat of August. I'd been making family dinners at night as if nothing had happened. Time had essentially collapsed. I was aware of my life, but all of it was tilted and seemed a different reality. Like the teal Atlantic Ocean wall, I wondered how much of my marriage had ever been real. If I hadn't found the emails, none of this would be happening. I would still be flailing and cursing about something that was wrong in our relationship that I just couldn't place, a feeling David kept telling me was wrong, a feeling I assumed was just me.

I understood the concept of growing apart in a marriage. I understood that I had changed. But when my husband told me we grew apart, and this is why the affair happened, an intense, blistering fuel traveled up my throat as if I had just inhaled gasoline. I had been suffering too. We were both there, in the marriage, together, the entire time. But I didn't fall in love with someone else. I defended our marriage and explained that we never grew apart. What does that even mean? I guess more than defending the relationship, I was defending the contract and the vow: Till death do us part.

When I check into the hotel, the man at the front desk asks me uncomfortably: "Only one room key?" I wish I could tell him I am with the bachelorette party checking in behind me. Boisterous and boa-covered, they move as one unit, as if riding on their own parade float covered in hot pink feathers.

"No, one key is fine," I answer, which seems to disappoint the young male desk clerk.

The trip is much lonelier than I thought it would be. In the cab on my way from the airport to the hotel, I realize my phone is about to die, and I can't find my charger. I remember packing it, checking that I had it, and rechecking for it, but after all that, I must have left it in the car. I take this as a terrible omen and react as if I'm in a war-torn country without fresh water or shelter. I call David with the remaining battery strength and explain that he won't be able to get hold of me all weekend. My voice is high and frantic, but he remains calm and unaffected on the other end, which incenses me even more. I get off the phone and feel the most pathetic and desperate I have ever felt, ever. Once checked in, I walk the two blocks to Walgreens, buy a bright pink charger for $17.99, and plug my phone in on the nightstand in my room. The lightning bolt in the top right corner of my screen immediately starts blinking. Crisis avoided, and my confidence rises. It's working! I fixed my phone charger problem! All that distress over nothing; all that inner turmoil, and I had the power to get a new phone charger the entire time.

My hotel room feels painfully quiet despite being on the Miami beachfront. There is a welcome note sitting between two perfectly etched rocks glasses and a golden brown bottle of scotch. The note simply says, "Relax!" and contains directions to the ice machine. I pick up one of the glasses and move it to the bathroom. The glass clinks when I set it on the white porcelain sink next to the faucet. I unpack my toothpaste and toothbrush and place them inside the fancy cup. I quit drinking six months ago. I consider calling the front desk to ask them to remove all the alcohol from the mini bar. But I don't.

At yoga on the hotel's roof deck the next morning, I stay bent over in baddha virabhadrasana—humble warrior pose, also meaning devotional warrior—and I'm reminded how easily I could give up. After all, the ground is right there for me to see and almost touch. I try not to think about David's girlfriend, Nicole. One finger, one hand, any little coming down from the pose will provide added comfort and support. I want relief from the constant pain of David's betrayal, and I consider numbing out with a drink. The temptation to access the mini bar is liquid and warm like the hot Miami sun. I want just the right amount of burn from the alcohol, like a sexy golden tan. No one would even know. And why does it matter anymore anyway? I thought by quitting drinking I would be saving my marriage. But since David is in love with someone else, does any of it even matter?

The morning ocean wind has died down, and the rising Florida heat fills my lungs with wet air as I breathe. I lunge further forward over my left leg and see my thigh muscles quiver next to the hem of my lightweight shorts. My clenched hands reach up and over, so the top of my head inches even closer toward my mat. The instructor paces, and I pull in my abdominals, an attempt to better disperse the weight. My breath expels, and my core wraps in all directions around my back. As my left quad muscles tire, my entire body wavers and sways. I can get out of the pose anytime. I can see the ground in front of me, and it begs me to touch it.

The moment that has been swirling through my head since finding the emails is the night several months ago when I asked David point blank if he was having an affair. "If you ever find out he just lied to you, you will leave . . ."

I remember my feet pressed on the cold hard tile of our kitchen, now eerily similar to my feet rooted into my mat. I remember David's playful face when he assured me I never had to worry. I remember my inner voice talking to me: *If you ever find out . . . you will leave . . .*

The instructor leads us out of humble warrior pose and back into warrior one for some relief. I grab the bottle of water from the front of my mat and, with my legs still spread in a wide lunge position, take a long gulping drink. Some of the water spills out from the bottle and wets my t-shirt. I lean forward onto my front leg in preparation for warrior three, our next pose in the series, and on my way forward I place the water bottle back on the ground, exactly where it was. After resetting the bottle, my body lifts immediately, and I reach my back leg straight out behind me. I square off my hips by tipping my right side slightly down, even though it wants to tilt up and open. I bring my hands into prayer position in front of my chest, and hold my core sturdy in the pose. The strength needed to stay in warrior three is a successful and welcome distraction from my busy mind.

The instructor invites us to extend our arms out in front of us, like Superman. I tighten my core muscles even more and pull up on the quadriceps in my standing leg. I begin to extend my arms out in front of me. I tip and tilt as I fly, not unlike a bird with open wings and a focused destination. I stretch through the heel of my floating leg and press it back firmly, as if there is a wall behind me. My body immediately reacts to the pressing energy, and my standing leg notices the support. I soften my shoulders and my triceps, which have hunched up to my ears, and allow their flesh to hang.

In some ways, flying in warrior three feels easy, much easier than bowing and being humble, much easier than fighting the ground's plea to just give up and touch it.

From warrior three the instructor asks us to mindfully lower our back leg and slowly tip our bodies upright, eventually bending our knee and lifting our foot in front of our torso for crane. I press my palms together tightly and bring them back to my heart center. I think of the rose quartz on my nightstand in my hotel room. I lift my crown to become upright, and as I lower my back leg, I carefully hover my foot an inch above my mat until bending my knee in front of me. Once standing, I open my arms out to the sides. In crane, I experience a different type of balance, a sturdy foundation on one leg. I close my eyes and breathe a renewing inhale and a relieving exhale in the hot August sun.

You said you would leave if you found out he lied. The voice emerges now that I have surrendered my mind and my body to the flow of the poses.

With a solid core, I move fluidly from bowing to flying to standing, and back to bowing. The adjustments are subtle. I am like the rolling waves from the ocean that move in to absorb debris from the shore, then drag it back out. My pores open under the blistering Miami sun and weep with the hot liquid of grief, pain, and truth. I have so many questions. If my husband doesn't love me, then does no one love me? As I send more pain and sadness out, there is still more to allow in. The last time I extend my body into warrior three, I watch tears drop heavily onto my yellow yoga mat. Or maybe it is sweat; beads of water trickle down between my breasts and wet my abdomen. Dampness takes over, and like the cleansing waves that wash across the shore, I cannot tell the difference between the liquid that is swelling from my skin and my own tears flowing freely out.

I return to my hotel room after rooftop yoga and text David. "I wish I had never married you."

I switch my phone to silent immediately after sending the text and sit at the foot of the bed to meditate. I cross my legs and tuck my ankles under my thighs. I root down in my seat and feel the hard hotel floor beneath me. I roll my shoulders back and away from my ears to lengthen my neck. I reach the crown of my head to the sky. I close my eyes. Anger wells up in my chest and creates a shallow, tight inhale. I shove the bitter sensation back down and try to expand my lungs. I glance at my phone and see that David has not written back. I close my eyes again and focus on my third eye, the center part of my forehead. After a few minutes, my breath eases and my lungs relax. My ribcage naturally allows for the inhale and the exhale, and my anger switches over to a deep sense of loss.

I open my mouth in resistance, but the tears arrive anyway. They stream down my cheeks and land at the top of my t-shirt. I continue to breathe through an open mouth and wonder when all the crying will stop. I don't like it. I touch my wet collar with my fingers and place my hands back in my lap. I lean my head against the mattress and squeeze my eyes shut so they can't open. Tears continue to sneak out, and I finally let them. My body lets go and I notice the voices of people and families enjoying the hotel pool below my room. I hear splashes of laughter and kids screaming in delight. I see only darkness behind my forehead.

Frustrated and unwilling to stay in meditation, I get up off the floor and crawl into the big white bed. I flop the air-conditioned covers heavily on top of me, roll into the coolness of the sheets, and close my eyes to sleep.

When I wake up, I check my phone still lying on the floor. Nothing from David. I look out the window and see the sky has turned pink. The pool is now quiet, and most of the lounge chairs that face the ocean are empty. A man and a woman sit close to each other and hold hands across their chairs. I see only their grasp and the top of the woman's sunhat, like a perfect photo from a vacation brochure.

I wonder why I came to Miami, why I came on this trip. The sadness is unbearable and not what I expected. Every other time I have been on vacation, the ocean and sunshine sustain and relax me. Despite the beautiful view, this trip is like punishment, and by far I am the loneliest I have ever been.

A little later, I drag my body out of bed and get dressed in a long flowing skirt and tank top. I do my hair and add red lipstick and black mascara. I try on one pair of shoes and look at myself in the full-length mirror. I remove the shoes and switch to a different pair. Satisfied with my reflection, I snap a photo. I consider sending the picture to David, but he still hasn't texted me back from earlier that day, and feeling pathetic, I decide not to. I walk down the stairs and out of my hotel to dinner. I sit in a booth alone and order a club soda when the server asks what I would like to drink.

"Just club soda?" he asks, like I'm required to order alcohol. How do people exist without alcohol?

"Yes," I answer.

I realize this is the new me and my future—just club soda and just one room key.

Ultimately, the warrior reminds us of the power of surrender. Balancing in warrior three requires as much surrender to the unknown as bowing in humble warrior requires faith in the solid ground. There is always energy to hold and sustain us even if we can't see it or physically touch it. Our jobs, our relationships, our status are all illusions of a safety net, while our inner self reflects our true capacity. Like every living thing, our real strength comes from inside of us. A wave is a wave and a human a human. I am not my marriage. I am not my job. I am not my titles or roles or daily tasks. Can I use my pain because it is here to teach me something, maybe about my capacity to expand my heart and my worth through adversity? Can I place my self-worth in myself, instead of someone else?

The next day I put on a short orange sundress and black running shoes. I strap my bag across my right shoulder and with my phone deep inside the pocket, I make sure my headphone cords reach my ears. I need music. I need to get out of my head.

I walk toward the beach and come upon a table covered in beautiful jewelry. A middle-aged woman and an older woman sit behind a colorful display of shimmering bracelets and necklaces. I can tell by their age and their appearance that they are mother and daughter. The daughter's hair is starting to gray around the front—she could be my mother. Her mother could be my grandmother with her silky white hair twisted up in a seashell clip and her small, fragile body. Their green eyes sparkle in the sunshine like the beaded jewelry they are selling. The older woman's cheek bones are a bit more pronounced than her daughter's, but the beaming smile and small front teeth match perfectly. Neither wears a wedding ring, and I imagine myself sitting behind a table of jewelry someday with my own mother—another glimpse at my future.

The tiny beads, intricately woven into rows, glisten under the morning sky, making them look more like jewels than plastic. Three sparkling bracelets catch my eye. Bright coral and rose gold beads alternate to create a striped pattern and are secured with shiny gold clasps at their ends. The three bracelets line up next to one another on the table and when I lay them over my wrist, it is obvious they should stay together. I won't be able to buy just one. The younger woman comes around from behind the table to help me fasten the clasps. She handles the bracelets one last time before sitting down and admiring how nice the orange and gold colors look on my tanned skin.

I make eye contact with the older woman, still sitting behind the table.

"You look so happy!" she exclaims. My heart knots up a little in my chest, like a wet towel being wrung.

"Isn't it a great feeling when you find exactly what you want?" The woman lowers her black sunglasses from the top of her head and sets them over her eyes, but does not look away from me.

"Yes," I answer, glancing down at the bracelets on my wrist. "I am very happy."

Saying the words out loud loosens the knot in my heart, and the heavy energy moves up into my throat. I am sad. I am lonely. I have been lonely for a long time. I am walking around with a broken heart, and maybe it has been broken for a long time.

I play each solution out in my head and I tense up at them all. Anger and denial are like rubbing alcohol on my already searing pain. Maybe I could stay if David changed his phone number. Maybe I could stay if David changed his job. Maybe I could stay if David changed his life, his self. An open and compassionate person would forgive, would be able to see that marriage is a two-way street, which means I am at fault too. So maybe his fault deserves understanding; maybe all faults are considered equal. Maybe I should stay.

I shove the knot down and out of my throat by swallowing and loosening my jaw. I drop the bills into the younger woman's hand and continue walking along the boardwalk. Calm ocean waves roll lazily up the sand, and families set up camps of beach towels, coolers, and umbrellas for the day. I rack my brain to find a solution, a reasonable adjustment that would rid me of this pain and allow our marriage to go back to the way it was. The new bracelets chime softly on my wrist as I swing my arm to my step and fight to discover a clever anecdote.

I wishfully pretend I could return home and David would tell me he is not in love with Nicole. He would tell me he missed me, and my trip would be validated. But he still hasn't texted me back from yesterday. I asked for space, and I guess he is giving it to me. I also wasn't very nice when I texted, telling him I never should have married him.

I keep walking on the wooden boardwalk. The song switches in my headphones, and I inadvertently start watching my feet in order to count my steps. Left right left right... One black tennis shoe darts forward and then the other. Left right left right... I feel like I am getting so small I am almost disappearing and no one will ever notice me or want me again.

I think that's why I like yoga and meditation so much, or walking on the boardwalk, being part of a crowded Miami beach, because I can be part of a group and still go inside. When I'm inside my own body, I am huddled and safe. I can observe the crowd but not let them see me, the broken, the bruised, the woman full of regret. Like the humble warrior, I bow over, defeated and wanting to die, but I am alive and here, and some inner strength I can't yet name keeps me hovering just above the ground.

TWENTY-TWO

A Return to Self

"Whatever we say there will always be at the back of
our minds the idea that if we try harder next time we
shall succeed in being completely good. Thus, in one
sense, the road back to God is a road of moral effort,
of trying harder and harder. But in another sense it
is not trying that is ever going to bring us home. All
this trying leads up to the vital moment at which you
turn to God and say, 'You must do this. I can't.'"

—C. S. Lewis

UTTANA SHISHOSANA

MY PALMS GRIP THE SLIPPERY MARBLE COUNTERTOP WHILE MY UPPER
body collapses down. My shoulder blades stretch as if in uttana
shishosana (puppy pose). My head dangles below my chest as I hang
on, possibly for dear life, to the edge of the counter. I don't want to fall
completely onto the kitchen floor, so I sob between gasps of breath and
watch my tears drop an entire leg's length down.

I returned from Miami and asked my husband of ten years to please move
out. "Please," I actually said when I looked at him. I can't handle living with a
man whom I know doesn't love me, a man I'll never be able to trust.

"It's OK. My mom can move back from Florida to help you with the
boys. I'll get an apartment nearby," he said.

A hot, spinning rage, like the blades on a toy helicopter, swirled
faster and faster in my stomach, just above my belly button, and the
force soon rose upward. The fiery ball gained heat and momentum as
it lifted through my chest cavity, my throat, and exploded out of my
mouth as a hot, unbelievable scream. No words. I could produce no
words. Embered residue rested on the tops of my cheeks and singed
their flesh like glowing ash. The reality of what my husband thought

of me overcame every cell in my body—I was his mother. I took care of children and prepared food. I drooled on my pillow when I finally fell asleep at night. I lost the carefree recklessness of single life when the only person to worry about was me. No wonder he didn't love me like a lover, like he used to.

David's mom and I got along like two cats fighting over the same spot in the sun. We circled one another and hissed, but then found ourselves entwined in a comfortable ring, both bodies able to be warmed, laying head to tail and tail to head, each of us sharing an equal half of the greater whole. Our similarities and our love for David and the boys became more evident the longer I was married. David's mom had been sober for twenty-two years, and when I decided to quit drinking, I marveled at the reality that our subconscious will always point us to the familiar. Like a fish that can't help but lurch for the bait, David had unknowingly married the same woman who put him through so much stress as a child. I felt responsible and wondered which came first: his mother, or my becoming her.

"What's wrong?" David had asked, when my reaction to his mother moving in with me came out as a fervored gasp.

"I want a husband. I don't want to be married to your mother."

David said that's not what he meant, but his words slammed into my gut like a tidal wave that lunged at the shore.

"How do you do it?" I texted my friend Sam. She had been sifting through more details of her husband's ten-year affair across the world. She grappled with what to do. One would think it might be easy. It was obviously justified if she just packed up and left. But when you've been with someone for that long and you've designed your life around their paycheck and their presence, it's not as easy to change as you'd think. A soul can be captured, slowly imprisoned by a rude comment here, a shifting of blame there, then beautiful flowers or great sex to make up for it. Insidiously, and over time, someone can be worn down, their confidence chiseled away until they think so little of themselves that they willingly stay in the cage because at least there they are fed and played with. They can't imagine how to survive without their captor, and it is better than being alone.

So when Tom traveled for work, Sam spent her time sleeping in fancy hotels and running on soft sandy beaches.

"How do you enjoy yourself?" I asked. Sam had just texted me a photo. She was smiling broadly in front of the ocean, holding her sandals in one hand as her other hand playfully grabbed at the hem of her dress. A purple-pink sun set majestically behind her.

"I find a stranger and ask them to take my photo. Then I smile the biggest smile ever. And I feel like I'm actually happy."

I hang off the edge of the counter and imagine my life without a marriage, without a lover, and without a companion. No one would ever want this abandoned drunk. My steady sobs enter a howling wail, and I bang repeatedly on the hard counter until my right palm bruises and flinches in pain. My head bobs up and down as my lungs grope for air. My inhale catches at the back of my throat, and my exhale bounces out like a skipping stone across a pond, the breath interrupted by the weight of my sobs.

My inner critical voice chastises loudly about how I could have been better, been more understanding of David's needs, not allowed this to happen. I pushed him away. He didn't love me. Maybe he never loved me. Maybe I was too difficult to love.

Aparigraha, "ungrasping," the fifth of the five yamas, usually requires a sufficient amount of suffering to finally enact. Like all the limbs, aparigraha needs to be practiced over and over again; letting go once does not mean we can't reattach to the form we so desperately think will save us. Unable to hold myself up any longer, I slide my hands all the way off the edge of the counter until I am in a small ball on the kitchen tile. I give in to the waves of sobs and cry ugly, obnoxious tears. My body shakes in release, like a wild animal meeting death. The convulsions and lack of control are so foreign to my body.

The next day I lay shaking in savasana at the end of my morning yoga class. I arrived open and at a loss, unable to sit alone in the house. I cannot do this alone. I have no idea how to do this. I pushed and forced my tired body through each pose during class and salivated the entire hour in anticipation of savasana where I could finally surrender my entire body to the floor and to the sky.

Down on my mat, I lift my chest off the floor and set it back down. I spread my shoulder blades flat and wide. I pick up and tense each leg and drop it back down with only gravity. I notice my heels hit the wooden floor beyond my mat somewhat loudly, and then my legs roll lazily onto the outer edges of my calves. I curl my fingers into fists and then let go so my arms and hands find heaviness like a lifeless corpse. I roll my head back and forth on the hard surface and hear the cracking sounds of skull crunching on hair. I imagine opening and spreading my scalp across the back of my mat, as if performing surgery. Legs open, arms open, chest exposed. I am on the operating table, and my heart whispers, *Take me, heal me, renew me. I don't like this current place.*

The soul exists inside the body and also in the sky. According to ancient Sanskrit texts called the vedas, Atman (true self) exists inside our solar plexus, right below our navel, and Brahman (universal truth) exists everywhere else. We are both Atman and Brahman. We are the drop and also the entire ocean.

My yoga teacher trainer and Kripalu faculty member, Yoganand Michael Carroll, said this to our class one day: "I inhale, the breath comes in; I exhale and I become the sky."

His words brought me home.

I used to lay on my back as a little girl on a sun-warmed blanket with my aunt and lose myself in the sky and moving clouds. We imagined shapes and figures and talked about what God wanted us to know. I wondered about the mystery of the heavens, and I wanted to be there, inside a cloud, seated next to God, and privy to all the divine secrets. My childhood mind always interpreted my body and my soul as separate from the divine. Heaven was always presented to me as a destination, if you were so lucky. But our soul exists both on the ground and in the sky. There is no destination; we ARE the sky.

Watching the sky as a girl, I glimpsed that I was not my body but something more. In savasana, I glimpse the same surrender. I observe the present moment more acutely because I realize there is nothing else for me to do. I'd rather not make a choice; I'd rather lay here and have everything taken away.

I inhale in savasana, and my body stops twitching and adjusting. A sense of peace descends over me, and I see puffy clouds travel slowly across my forehead beneath my closed eyes. I am near God, just like I always wanted. I feel a heaviness on my right shoulder, like a warm hand, and it nudges me just enough to feel safe. OK, I think. Maybe I can do this. Like the clouds gliding by inside my forehead, I see a moment outside myself and a life outside the cage. I see a moment of possibility.

If you've been faced with something traumatic or even disappointing, there is a point when you finally let go. You stop squirming and resisting and admit that you need help. You release control and enact faith, both in something bigger than yourself and in a divine path selected just for you. This type of surrender often becomes desirable only after something so unbelievable and so earth-shattering occurs that you have no choice but to renounce everything you've ever known. My happy marriage, my perfect appearance, my well-put-together life.

You want today to be the last day. The last day you wake up and pretend to have control over outside circumstance. You cannot hide toxicity, abuse, and dysfunction behind new cars and kids' birthday parties. The reality that my life was not as I had carefully put it together, that the surface did not match the depths, shocked me. Meditation brings us to the depths; with practice, we can quiet the outside distractions in order to loosen and unravel their grip on our sense of self.

When the pain is so acute, giving it away to something outside ourself may be the only act that brings relief. We release the idea that the circumstance defines us in order to withstand it. I smiled during breakfast with the boys, and I projected some sort of image that our life was still in tact. But inside, I had given up. Inside, I had surrendered to something outside of myself. My faith that I was not alone, that this situation was not the truth about me removed my burden, made me curious, and eventually carried me through to the other side.

AGNISTAMBHASANA

The tiny fire Cait and I made one summer during high school jumped even higher on her parents' gravel driveway when we added the soft paper letters. My now ex-boyfriend's handwriting was thin and slanted, like the blonde, wispy hairs that snuck out from my French braid. I watched the pale blue lines and my handwritten name curl up under burning orange embers, turn black, then white, and eventually float up as ash before disappearing into the crisp, fall sky.

In India, yagna refers to a sacred fire; it's the Sanskrit word for sacrifice, worship, or offering. The sacred offering is done with accompanying mantras and holy chanting. At sixteen, Cait and I had no idea that our high school burning ritual actually had legitimate roots, that by offering our ex's love letters to the sky, we might be releasing the trauma of a broken summer romance. We had engaged in this ritual many times before, burning any keepsake or memory immediately after a break-up. We burned letters, photos, dried corsages, even silky prom dresses, anything and everything in order to symbolize our willingness to let go and move on.

After I drop the boys off at school, I drive to Tyler's yoga class, hoping to relieve my mind of the thoughts and busyness surrounding what I perceive to be my failed marriage. I want to retreat to my mat. I want to forget. Toward the end of class, Tyler tells us we are moving into agnistambhasana (fire log pose), which I have never done before, but I like the name. There is only one other student in class today besides me, a man named Jim. While seated, I place my right leg parallel to the front of my mat, like instructed, which is the same way we set up for pigeon pose. Tyler demonstrates how we should stack our left leg on top of the right, and make sure our knees and our shins line up evenly, just like stacking wood for a fire.

I wince as I angle my front leg parallel to the top edge of my mat. I lift my left leg and place it on top of my right, but when I do, my left knee pops up. I inhale and exhale deeply and coax my left knee down a little more with my palm.

Trees outside the window already drop red and yellow leaves. As the unusually warm September air wafts through an open door, I smell the burning letters from almost twenty-five years ago.

Opening the hip flexors releases physical as well as emotional pain. Aware of the burning sensation in my hips, my legs behave whimsically in the pose, like a random pile of sticks being tossed carelessly onto a pile. Not at all like neatly stacked logs for a proper fire, my legs appear more like kindling; they fall and dangle around the edges.

I look over at Tyler and Jim. Their fire logs nest perfectly on top of one another and their spines are erect. They both breathe steadily and comfortably, with their eyes gently closed. I squint my eyes and judge them, and an ache erupts from behind my heart. I wonder what I did to cause my husband's affair. I wonder why the summer boyfriends always left. I wonder at my inability to let go and my desire to hold on so tightly.

I've been told by several yoga teachers that women hold pain and trauma in their hips and jaws. Actually, the two are connected, so when draping forward in pigeon pose or standing sideways in warrior two, I always remember to unclench my jaw to help relieve the uncomfortable sensation in my hips and in hopes of releasing the stuck energy. Often while in hip opening poses, actual tears spring to my eyes as if someone has just lit a match close to a deeply buried wound, seared off the scab, and brought it bloody to the surface.

I am still trying to get my knee flat on top of my bottom leg. My hips bones sting from the seated position. I press gently with my hands and breathe, but the burning sensation deep inside my hip sockets persists. I release my jaw and inhale again. My thigh muscles are now weary, so my knees flutter and shake upward, like the paper and fabric Cait and I tossed into our fires. I think of my husband's infidelity and the heartache of past relationships. The more I breathe and the more I press down on my knee, the more tenderness floats to the surface.

Compassionately, I release some of the pressure with my palms, and accept my position. I stop comparing myself to Tyler and Jim and close my eyes. Slight pain still seeps into my bones, but I am not hanging on to the sensation so tightly. I stop grasping at something that was never mine in the first place. I release the gripping in my toes and allow them to curl comfortably under my natural weight. Miraculously, I begin to sink closer to the ground. My crown reaches upward, seeking clarity and forgiveness. The pain in my legs squeezes out an awareness that I am not OK, which goes directly against my pattern and my instinct to declare the opposite. *I am fine* is my daily mantra.

"I'll always love you, Molly," said my husband after he told me he was in love with another woman.

"I'll always love you, Molly," said my high school boyfriend seconds after he broke up with me. Twenty years later he said it to me again when I ran into him shortly after his second wedding. At his words, my heart jumped like a flickering flame, a tiny pilot light in my chest that had never burned out.

"What?" I asked. Mark shrugged and smiled. "You know what I mean. It's all just timing." The contradiction confused and angered me, but I smiled and said thank you as if his statement was all I deserved. If someone loves me, don't they want to stay? Am I asking for too much from love?

I have trouble letting go, letting the pricks and pain completely release. Burning love letters and mementos has always scared me because who am I once I let the relationships go? Part of me wants to savor the grief and taste the sour heartache just so I don't completely forget what it's like to be in love.

The longer we sit in the uncomfortable pose, the longer I allow my hips to scream and my knees to inch closer down. I am lighter and not as judgmental of my stance. I envy Tyler and Jim and their ease in the pose, their supposed ability to move on from trauma willingly and quickly, as if it never happened. But I also feel deep compassion and even gratitude for my own pain, and my burning hips feel not like a punishment or a permanent place but instead offer me an invitation to succeed and to transcend.

After yoga, I arrive home and begin burning evidence of my marriage in the stone fireplace in our living room. Soon, the wedding cards, anniversary cards, letters from my and David's early dating, poems, and photographs have all been burned. The heat from the fireplace mingles with the fiery, end-of-summer air floating in through the open window. I participate in yagna as an attempt to dismantle the past, to dramatically and fully release myself from the entanglement of my marriage. I not only want out of the marriage, I want out of the fire, the burning that creeps up my spine as soon as I discover an overlooked photograph tucked inside a drawer.

Despite my burning ceremony, old cards and photos wait for me inside boxes and the pages of books, and I discover them the second I am caught off guard. I can't find every shred of evidence of our marriage and burn it all. I can't force my knees down or my hips open. I can't expect that there will never again come a day when I won't be hit with the avalanche of pain and grief that comes from love. Yoga does not promise that we will avoid pain and tenderness, but rather that we will be able to open ourselves to these emotions to learn about ourselves and our potential.

When we disown our emotions, we disown parts of our self. Meditation invites us to sit down and feel, rather than run away. Meditation asks us to find our breath, our life force, and send it to the places that have been begging for our attention.

Meditation teaches us how to look in, instead of out, and begins our much needed love affair with self.

PATITA TARASANA : FALLEN STAR

PART VIII

Samadhi : Enlightenment

I AM

"Have you ever had a dream that you were certain was real, only to wake up and realize that everyone and everything in the dream was really you? Well this is how many mystics describe the nature of our reality, as a dream in which we think we are individual personalities existing in the physical universe. But eventually, like in all dreams, we will wake up. Except in this dream we do not wake up to realize we are still in the world, we awake from the world to realize that we are God."

—Joseph P. Kauffman

The Eighth Limb, Samadhi, is Enlightenment, possibly the end-goal of our entire yoga practice. What is enlightenment? Who has it and what does it feel like? Truthfully, I am not there; I know I have glimpsed freedom through my practice, and to me, this is as close to liberation from suffering as I will get.

We can practice living Samadhi by trusting and honoring who we are. To be who we are requires self acceptance, a small tilt of your head towards your heart; your own heart holds the answers. Your own heart is where God lives, where love lives, and where all the truth of our oneness resides.

Enlightenment is available to everyone; it's available to you too. You only let yourself believe you are a victim to external factors. Everything you have ever needed has been inside you the whole time. God is inside you. Love is inside you. You've held the power all along.

TWENTY-THREE

Love Stories

"Love did reign. Love does reign. Love still reigns."

—Nausicaa Twila

JUNE 2009

THERE'S NO GOOD PLACE TO DISCREETLY BREASTFEED A BABY IN A CAR dealership. So while David continued to negotiate our trade-in with the young man wearing a royal blue polo shirt and khaki pants, I went to the bathroom. Once in the stall, I sat down on a toilet seat, hard and slippery against my sundress. There was no lid to put down, so the hole in the middle made it impossible to lean back or relax my body comfortably. I felt like I would fall in at any moment. I pulled down the strap of my dress from my shoulder and undid the clasp on my nursing bra. I quietly sang to our new baby Bennett who was screaming and directed his infant face toward my breast. The echoing room became immediately silent as he filled his mouth and began to suck. My nipple stung with pain from our amateur latch, but my body relaxed in the silent isolation of the stall.

We had been browsing and haggling over a car for the last three hours with our new, two-week-old baby. The dealership was having a tailgate-like party in their lot outside. Music pounded from the speakers in the parking lot and the smell of sizzling burgers and hot dogs traveled temptingly through the air. Shiny new cars gleamed in the Sunday afternoon sunshine while colorful balloons celebrated the possibility of being able to drive one home. The crowd chattered with excitement as they wandered leisurely among the sparkling paint and shiny, mirrored wheels. They sipped cans of soda and ate from small, crinkling bags of chips.

By the time I peeled myself away from the long-winded salesman who loved the sound of his voice, Bennett had been warning me with gentle whines, which turned into long cries and then persistent, hungry screams. I was the only woman in the entire car lot and the only one who noticed the baby at all. Three hours of not eating might as well have been three days. I was sweating more and more at the escalation of each cry. My heart raced and I scanned the showroom for couches or any seating useful to feed the baby. I searched out a quiet corner, or a hidden chair. I thought of slinking into the backseat of one of the cars, but decided on the bathroom as my best option.

Forty-five minutes later, achy and stiff from holding my body upright on the toilet, I emerged with the now sleeping baby. I walked to the man's desk and sat down in a chair next to David. While I was gone, they had decided on a final price and were already signing the papers.

The night before, I hugged David and pressed my entire form into his because I wanted to disappear into his body. The pent-up exhaustion and fear released inside of me, and I prayed for his weight and strength to hold me through new motherhood. Tears wet his t-shirt as I pleaded with him, "What if I can't do this? What if I can't be a mom?" His arms wrapped all the way around my small frame. He squeezed my shoulders tightly, "You're a great mom. You can do this. Everything will be fine, I promise. I love you."

"I love you too." I let go, wiped my face, and went to check on the baby.

FEBRUARY 2018

"Go out and celebrate after. Buy yourself a glass of champagne." My friend Natalie from Los Angeles tells me on the phone a few days before my divorce hearing. Natalie and I haven't known each other that long, so she is unaware that I don't drink. I let myself hang on the thought a little too long; my tongue tingles in anticipation of the bubbles rising familiarly to my head. I sigh an audible exhale. "Ahhhh, that's a good idea," I respond. A celebration.

I am anxious for February 13. I have been anxious ever since I received the eighty-four-page stack of papers sent in an orangish envelope from my attorney, which I found angled sideways inside my mailbox because the size didn't exactly fit. I undid the red string at the top of the envelope and peeled back the seal. The first page was a letter with instructions. "Sign where you see the yellow tabs. The court date is set for February 13, which is non-negotiable, so make sure you both can be there."

I flipped to the next page: "To dissolve the marriage of Molly Jean Chanson Addison to David Scott Addison, married August 19, 2006. Molly Jean Chanson Addison to restore her maiden name (Chanson). On the basis that the marriage is determined to be irretrievable."

Irretrievable and restore. Weighted words. One holds the assumption that something has been lost and traveled too far out of reach. Like a bottle washed away from shore, the marriage was now unsalvageable. Without risking self-injury or death, there's no way to swim far enough or deep enough in order to bring back what once was. But then the word restore indicates breath and life and an ability to come back, like an artist who painstakingly dusts off the residue of an abandoned painting to reveal the gold flecks and careful detail underneath. Restoration removes the neglected and possibly damaged surface, and the painting becomes beautiful once again. Desired instead of discarded.

Irretrievable made me wince, like the broken promise of love was my own heart that would never grow back. How irretrievable am I? I remembered when my lawyer asked if I would like to return to my maiden name, my name before marriage, my name before tying myself to another's identity. A yellow sticky tab shaped like an arrow pointed to the line I needed to sign. I grabbed the pen from the counter and signed, a promise, and a first step in my own restoration.

On February 13 I wear loose-fitting black pants and a gray turtleneck sweater, as if I were going to a job interview. I wear comfortable, quiet shoes that don't click when I enter the cement and tiled building. After I pass through the metal detector and retrieve my bag and hefty divorce document, I head upstairs to a small room where I have agreed to meet my attorney. She runs me through the process, what the judge will ask me and how I should respond. She notices that I am nervous and explains that she will do most of the talking, not to worry.

The courtroom hums with soft whispers and shuffling papers. I see David sitting in the second row, and he turns to look at me when he hears the heavy, squeaking door amidst the silence. At first I float toward him like a lost bottle bobbing toward land, but before I sit down, the judge enters from a side door and takes her place behind the large, platformed desk. She glances at her clipboard and immediately calls our names. We all make our way up and walk through a short, swinging door that divides the front of the courtroom from the general seating. We sit at opposing desks and my attorney begins the proceedings, announcing that we are all present.

My attorney reads through the script, and the judge obliges and responds. During their back and forth, I stare at David. He is crying. He looks at me like he hasn't in a really long time, and his eyes billow with redness. But I feel no pang in my chest this time, no urgent desire to go to him. I watch his eyes well up and notice his tears activate no similar welling up inside my own body. I am concentrating too hard on my lines.

David answers the judge and tells her he agrees to let the kids stay with me 72 percent of the time. He agrees to make the child support payments. He agrees to always keep a life insurance policy. He agrees to provide the boys with health insurance. He agrees to never ask me for anything financial, no matter my situation. He says "I do" more times than at our wedding.

Then it is my turn. "I do." "It is." "Yes." "Yes." "I do."

I wonder if anything could go wrong. It has slipped my mind that I am actually waiting for a ruling and that the judge does not have to grant this divorce. I have no evidence. How does she know we have really worked on it? That the marriage is in fact, irretrievable?

"By the State of Wisconsin, divorce is granted." Bang, her gavel lands affirmingly on the hard mahogany surface, and she calls the next name on her clipboard.

I look at David and he wipes a tear from under his eye. A heat the size of a pilot light clicks on inside my chest and travels up to my eyes. I glance at my attorney through the soft burning sensation, and she nods to me that it is complete. In the hallway, I say goodbye to David and tell him I'll drop the boys off in two days. We stand for a moment, unable to touch each other and unsure how to part. Irretrievable is now a gap we will hang out in together, standing at the shore, watching the waves rush in and out. I know my marriage has been swept away, but I need to stare out a little longer just to be sure.

I get out to my car and sit for a moment in the front seat before putting the key in the ignition. I think of the two bottles of pink champagne I had purchased on my way to the court house, stashed inside their paper bags, and nestled together inside a larger paper bag, all hidden beneath the floor mat in the trunk of my car. I bite my lower lip and unwind the winter scarf around my neck that now threatens to strangle me. I start the car, turn up the heat and the music, and drive home.

The releasing pop of the first champagne bottle the day of my divorce finally stops my hands from shaking like they have the entire car ride home. I get out one of the two silver stemmed champagne glasses David and I got as a wedding gift, the only barware I hadn't smashed and thrown away after quitting drinking as a defiant symbol of the wreckage my life had become. I pour the effervescent liquid into my glass, and delicious pink bubbles rise to tickle my nostrils. With a delicate grip but a steady hand, I lift the hopeful silver stem, place the glass to my lips, and take a sip.

I smile and convince myself I deserve this. I deserve a drink. Anyone would do the same if they were me. Maybe now that all of this is behind me—my marriage, the affair, and the divorce— I can handle drinking again, this time as a normal, happy person. I just want to feel worthy, like the five-year-old me who pretended to drink and smoke on Grandma's fencepost. I take another sip and look around. Nothing happens. I take another sip and another, until my body lightens and the corners of my mouth turn up. My eyelids soften. I have missed this feeling of dulled out thoughts, a world full of easy, rounded edges rather than harsh angles.

To this day, I don't have the answer for my relapse, or for the two that came after that until I decided to get more help. I could easily say I felt sorry for myself, but I sense it is more complicated than that. Addiction is physical, like diabetes or asthma, because an organ of the body lets us down. In the case of addiction, the brain. Once we remove the alcohol or substance, our brain returns to normal function. But addiction is also emotional. In yoga, the emotional body is referred to as the subtle body and includes beliefs that lie underneath our physical form, habits that form behind our rational mind, and our overall sense of self, which might take root by the time we are five years old.

By the end of the bottle, the hopefulness of being able to drink vanishes into a dark knowing of despair, shame, and loneliness. Deep, deep loneliness. Only this time is much worse because I know I have broken a vow to myself. I know everyone at my meetings and my therapy are right; the first drink will undo me, like one pull on the string, and I won't be able to stop.

I go through both bottles and then go out to get more, hiding them in the same spot in my car, cushioned quietly inside two paper bags, before picking up my boys from school. I consider not drinking them; the mere presence of the ready-to-pop bottles beneath the secret compartment in the trunk gives me comfort, like an extra layer of clothing if I am to be stranded in a bad storm. Of course the storm has already begun, and I do retreat back to the car, late that night, to finish the evidence. The next day I arrive in a puddle of self-loathing on my bathroom floor.

I relapse two more times after my divorce, each time providing me with more insight into addiction, relapse, and recovery. After every binge, I pick myself up, endure the tremors that take hold of my body for days after I remove the poison, at which point I tell myself I cannot do this again; I cannot watch my body crash and wreck into shore like an unmanned ship. I don't have the getting-back-up in me.

Maybe the turning point is when we enact the fifth niyama, ishvara pranidhana, and we finally surrender to who we are. Instead of trying to drink again, to fit in, or to mold myself into a societal norm, instead of wearing the mask of perfection and beauty, my relapses all taught me to admit the looming darkness inside myself.

My last drink is a glass of room temperature white wine I find rolling around beneath my bed. I start researching rehabs and pack my bags.

JULY 2018

I stare out the passenger seat window on a bright sunny summer day. Highway and billboards zip by, dotted with the occasional tree. I shouldn't be here, riding in the car with my parents on a Thursday morning, the day after the Fourth of July, exactly one year after finding the emails from David's girlfriend, Nicole. The boys have swim lessons today. Jen's mom has agreed to take them since I cannot.

I know from the photos on the treatment center's website that we will be entering through a large, black gate at the end of a long, tree-lined driveway. Still, when we arrive and my dad gives my name to the intercom, I feel a lurch in my stomach and exhale a long breath through my open mouth. The wrought-iron arches part in the middle and we drive through. I briefly close my eyes and try to remember who I am. When I open them, I see the large white house sitting on a hill to the left, the strong, wooden door, the large columns on either side, and the whole visual experience feels not unlike arriving at a mental institution. Insanity tucked neatly away in the countryside, the inability to handle life masked by a gently rushing waterfall and freshly cut grass.

"Maybe this is a mental institution?" I say inquisitively because I know we are all thinking the same thing. Two white Adirondack chairs sit on the lawn near a pond at the front of the house. I watch a small bunny bound into the tall reeds as our car winds further up to the property.

"Well, that's good." My dad responds. "There's obviously something mental going on."

My mind strays from its daydreamy thoughts, and I am bluntly reminded of why we are here. My dad does not daydream; he likes practical solutions. And in his mind, this is a solution, a cure for all my unexplainable behavior that has surfaced since my divorce. The excessive drinking. The depression. The inability to just get over my husband's affair and stay positive, to "pull myself up." My behavior demonstrates an inability to cope in a rational and presentable way, which points to an obvious unwillingness to let go and move on.

I look at treatment as a savior, a place I can finally be myself, share my deepest secrets, and not have anyone judge me. A place where I am allowed to feel things and show things and cry about things. A place that will protect me and heal me. A place where I can safely throw up all the pain and expel it from my body, like an ocean wave tossing garbage on its shore.

I get out of the car and walk up to the front door of the treatment center. I adjust my t-shirt and touch my hair. I don't have to knock because the facility is expecting me. The door opens, and I remember the paper I signed to be here on which I circled all my symptoms and check-marked what I thought to be my disease.

As terrifying as it is to leave everything that matters in my life temporarily behind, part of me is relieved to step away from the world and actually focus on myself. The rippling creek and tall grasses that decorate the front lawn of the treatment center call to me like home, and tell me, just for now, for these five weeks, to let everything go, and be here in the present.

Rehab is like a walking meditation, a long yoga practice, and an endless savasana. I ride the waves of intense emotion, grueling work, painful insight, and uncomfortable stillness, but I also experience ethereal lightness, emotional release, reassuring strength, and an abiding faith in myself. My path to recovery begins when I set aside how I want to look in front of everyone else, and I claim the intention to discover myself from wherever I left off.

I have been sober ever since. Life is not a straight line. Sobriety is not a straight line. To captain our own ship is not to avoid the mast splitting in storms, the hull scraping along jagged rock, or the bow crashing into unintended land. Our structure is not meant to sail through unscathed. The journey brings constant upheaval and inevitable damage, all which hold the lessons and the tools for healing and repair.

Like the eight limbs of yoga teach us, the goal is not enlightenment, with nothing to worry about once we achieve it. To glimpse enlightenment is to witness our wholeness, despite dark pasts, and our constant held-ness within the divine. This is why yoga is a practice; we must return again and again, to our mat, to our heart, and to our inner teacher, so we can make the next best choice. Often it takes a perfect storm for a total collapse to occur. Just like my alcoholism and my husband's infidelity came to light during the same, catastrophic year, they also healed one another at the same time. Lessons overlapped, truths about myself and my fears became more accessible. I witnessed the eight limbs in all aspects of my recovery—non-violence, self-study, truth, and surrender. The perfect storm that brought me to the bathroom tile became the perfect catalyst for radical change and healing.

DECEMBER 2018

The man at the tree lot this year helps us tie our Christmas tree to the top of the car. It's only me and the boys now, and we can't lift it ourselves. The man points out the magic string, the one that needs to be pulled when we get home, that will effortlessly undo all the knots.

After completing my treatment in August, I am barely six months sober. I am terrified to endure another holiday of clinking glasses and Aquavit shots; the bottle of grain alcohol frozen inside a block of ice and decorated with slices of orange and sprigs of dill is a Swedish tradition in my family. But I get through it, not easily and not without doubting myself along the way. Every time I come home from a party or holiday event, I thank God (my understanding of divine support) for helping me through. Somehow, magically, this makes all the difference. By enacting faith and by trusting myself, I release the burden of needing to know all the reasons why. Why I have this addiction, why my husband cheated, why I am on this path. I have spent my whole life questioning my path and whether or not it is right. I mistakingly assume unruly seas mean I am doing something wrong, that I have aimed my bow toward the wrong shoreline. I learn that all I have to do is let go of that expectation. Nothing is painless. nothing is without curling tides and threatening horizons. As Pema Chödrön reminds me, "The path is the goal," and learning to right the ship is part of the deal.

"In the chaotic rubble, she still remembered who she was."

I picture a woman whose house has just been blown away in a hurricane. She stands alone on the shore after the storm, among debris, fallen trees, and broken glass. Splintered wood and lost possessions float aimlessly on the ocean's surface, and the woman wonders how to retrieve and put everything back together.

There is another woman who stands in her own living room, toys and books scattered around, and the baby finally asleep after a long and anxious day.

And finally, there is a woman who crawls under the covers at night, warm yet exhausted by fear, a woman who just found out her child has a disability, a woman who cares for her small children and her aging parents at the same time, a woman who fights her own illness or addiction while still working and raising a family. We are all this woman. We all have weathered our own storms, and the pelting rains grant us access to who we are, deep down, at our indestructible center.

Who we are is resilient. Despite anything we are going through, I see women every single day who show up in spite of their circumstances. We show up despite losing all our hair to chemo, we show up after finding out our partner of ten years has a lover, we show up tired and confused, but with cookies, stews, and a smile on our face.

I sense the solid wall behind me while in headstand, the energy of its form a reliable safety net. When my legs have completely risen to the top, now directly above my hips, my chest, and my shoulders, this is when balance really threatens me. I have arrived, but only just recently. I immediately start shaking at the realization that I am actually in headstand. The instructor yelps, "Great job, Molly!" But I don't feel like celebrating yet. My core shakes. My shoulders ache. My neck burns. I stretch my fingers because I realize they are so tightly clenched; I am afraid to let any amount of grip go.

I inhale and exhale. In the inversion, I do not close my eyes. My mom always told me not to close my eyes while upside down because it would make me dizzy. I get my bearings in headstand. I see the mat upside down in my eyesight. I see the wall across from me and a tree losing its leaves outside the window. Something loosens, and my feet feel more like they are floating than reaching. My shoulders drop down my back despite being upside down, and my body simultaneously lifts.

I don't think we go low just to stay there or to be punished. I think we go low in order to understand our ability to rise.

There is a preciousness to journeys that are hard—new motherhood, new recovery, new divorce, death, and loss. A bittersweet memory attaches to every new beginning and every next step forward. We cling to difficult moments in the past because we remember the sweetness of surrender. In moments of chaos and confusion, faith steps in, not necessarily tied to a religion, but rich with a spirituality and a concept greater than I. An understanding that something else is carrying us when we need it most. We operate on a different plane, an adjacent wavelength, because we sense that there is a wall behind us, and that we are being held. This is always the case, but for some reason when life is good, we forget.

Our conditioning and our culture train us to believe pain is a bad thing, and when we feel it, we should make it go away. Yet life continually shows me over and over again that my most painful times are also the most beautiful and by far the most meaningful. These are the times I have the opportunity to let go in order to evolve, to surrender like the caterpillar inside her tight and stifling chrysalis so that she can allow for the uncomfortable but necessary transformation into a butterfly.

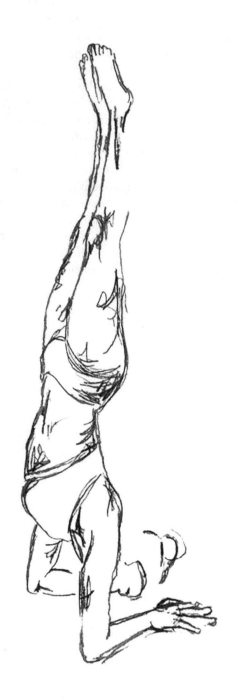

PINCHA MAYURASANA : FOREARM STAND

TWENTY-FOUR

Dharma

"When you make a choice, you change the future."

—Deepak Chopra

STRENGTH POSE

WHAT IS THE PRICE OF YOUR INTEGRITY? IN YOGA PHILOSOPHY, WE achieve enlightenment by seeking our dharma, our essential nature, our function of being, and our sacred duty. The path to seek dharma is not linear; we must follow our energy, trust our feelings, and be honest about our intention. Are we living for ourselves or for others? Are we behaving in our true nature or acting out the dharma of someone else? Unlike actions that stem from jealousy, comparison, or a need to prove, actions taken in the pursuit of dharma will transform us because our soul's purpose serves the greatest good, the collective consciousness as well as the individual.

A year and a half after my divorce, twenty-five years after doing my first yoga practice with my mom in our living room, I finally enroll in the yoga teacher training from the catalog that had peskily nagged at me along my entire life's path.

The final yoga class I attend as a student at Kripalu, after the month-long immersion, is in the third-floor studio at 7:00 a.m., the morning of our graduation. I stand in parshva virabadhrasana, side warrior pose, and the instructor tells us to bring our outstretched arms in toward our heart on the inhale, then straighten them back out fast and make a "whoosh" sound out of our mouth on the exhale. I inhale and bring my arms in, then exhale loudly, "Whooooosh!"

We repeat the movement several more times, and with each forceful exhale, I think of the last year and a half—my divorce, my one year sober anniversary, and the absurdity of life, the fact that my mom unknowingly handed me the Kripalu catalog back when I was in high school.

On the final exhale with my arms reaching wide, we turn our feet to face out and squat down slowly into malasana. Once my hands touch the wooden floor, I naturally lean my body forward, press my palms firmly into the earth, and place my knees onto the backs of my forearms. I tip forward into crow, a balance and strength pose. I had forgotten about crow pose until now. I hadn't done the pose since a few summers before when I was outside on warm, soft grass, when I still didn't know about David's affair. That day, I had leaned too far forward as my gaze chased a butterfly onto a rosebush, and I crashed, unable to catch myself. I fell swiftly and beautifully onto my chin. I remember my teacher's instruction that day: "Don't look down. Keep looking straight ahead."

During the Kripalu class, I lift my head just enough to gaze at the unmoving edge of my friend Abby's mat in front of me. I hold steady and strong in the balance, focused and unwavering. I continue to take full complete breaths and notice how completely different I feel from the day I was distracted, afraid to fall, and tumbled out of the pose. The memory makes my heart swell, for that woman, for that profound time, until the beating organ fills up my chest like a cloud expanding with rain, and when my body can no longer contain the heaviness, tears pour out of my eyes, hitting the wooden planks beneath my chin. I crack wide open, and surprisingly, for the first time, the openness doesn't feel like it will kill me. Cracking open, breaking, and enduring the sharp edges actually makes me feel more whole. I can stretch my branches over the cliff and still stay rooted to the ground. My inner voice speaks to me, "You are returning to your life as a whole person."

I tip backward until my toes touch the ground, and I sit down out of the pose. I fold my arms on top of my knees and hang my head between them. Pieces of me hadn't come back together because the pieces were always there. I was only living enough to step around them. Like a shattered glass left on the floor, I gingerly avoided the mess, too afraid to deal with it and clean it up. Over the last few years, I learned that my life is my responsibility. I learned I can be true to myself. I learned I can accept myself and stop seeking so much approval. I learned that the lesson is not to keep my heart intact, but to continue opening, even after every break. Breaking makes me human; breaking means I exist.

To achieve samadhi we recognize that we are divine, that every circumstance we are faced with is a holy encounter and an opportunity to heal. Healing then is not so much fixing ourselves, like we think of when we break a bone or get sick. Healing the soul is not mending or recovering because nothing is wrong or broken in the first place. Healing the soul is a return to what we already are, to the parts of ourselves we have forgotten or abandoned as a result of misinterpreting our experiences.

We can practice living samadhi by trusting and honoring who we are, at our core, regardless of conditioned habits, regardless of false beliefs, and regardless of someone else's actions toward us. Living an enlightened life means that every decision you make is done from a place of love and compassion, and honors your true self. What you eat for breakfast, whether or not you quit your job, how you parent, how you pray, how you spend your time, all if it reflects your relationship to yourself. And you already possess what you crave. Your longings are not a mistake or a coincidence; your longings are meant for you.

To my amazement and wonder, the love I have been searching for my entire life to save me has been inside my own heart the entire time.

Sacred duty can be misperceived as something famous or life-altering. But we all are here with a sacred duty—to honor our soul's calling. Dharma is available to everyone, not just Buddha or Ghandi or Martin Luther King, Jr. Maybe your calling is motherhood or caregiving, a profession or a pastime. This state of living who you are comes from inside of you and has little to do with what your life looks like on the outside.

To pursue our sacred duty and to practice the eighth limb of yoga, we ride the waves of life, of loss, of tragedy, and of joy. To pursue your sacred duty is to discover who you are, through deep inner acknowledgment rather than an external view. If dharma refers to anything that transforms us, our entire life experience becomes our path. Every adversity becomes an opportunity. Every pain point leads us to truth and enlightenment. You are practicing yoga always.

DANDASANA

I stand in line at the DMV, to change my last name from married back to maiden. I hate saying back because I am not traveling backward, I am moving forward.

Luckily the process at the DMV has a form. Papers sit on the pale gray counter stacked in a wire basket with a label in clearly typed black font that says, NAME CHANGE. I hand my completed form to the heavy set, scruffy man behind the counter. "Hi!" I say, probably too excitedly for everyone else at the DMV, except the sixteen-year-olds who are there to get their license for the first time. The man has a nice smile, so his gruff voice alarms me when he speaks.

He eyes my name change form and then glances at my face and down my body. The man asks, "How many times have you been divorced?" His question is loud, and I know everyone in line behind me and within the small square room can hear.

"Just once." I answer, but for some reason my cheeks burn and I pull my shoulders back and down in order to become taller. I lean slightly toward him and continue to maintain eye contact.

The man has no reaction and keeps looking at me. I hold my gaze steadily with his. I do not smile or cough or twitch. Steady gaze.

"Just once." I repeat.

"OK," he finally replies, "because you can only change your name so many times. There's a limit."

I smile again. "That's fine," I answer. "I'm not going to make this a habit." The man does not smile back. I don't think he likes my joke. Or maybe he doesn't trust me as I stand there in my denim jacket and red suede sneakers. I probably look like I should be here with a parent, like I could be taking the driving test myself.

I sigh and hope to get this over with, hope the man will take my form and complete the process, but he continues. "So flying—when flying you'll have to bring your ID as well as your marriage and divorce certificate, every time, just to be safe. They check everything now and they're always changing the rules. Eventually they're going to make everyone travel with a passport, even within the United States. I would always bring any record of a name change with you, just to be safe."

He ends his long lecture, and I stand there. I don't say anything because he hasn't asked for my opinion. I don't understand why I need proof of my marriage or proof of my divorce just to fly across the country, or to do anything. I realize in this moment that by taking my name back, something is being unrooted. A core belief is being dug into, and it might not sit well with everyone.

I no longer like this man. I no longer want to stand in line and pretend to be nice for the sake of non-confrontation. Who the fuck is this guy? And fuck him! I can change my name to anything I want, and it's none of his fucking business why I do or don't. I'm not asking him how he ended up working at the DMV or how many relationships he's had. My life is none of his business, and his sexist, judgmental energy pisses me off.

I wish I had mustered the courage to say something while standing in front of him, but I stick to the form.

"Is my form OK? Do you need something else?" I glance at the paper in his hand.

"You'll need to get a new social security card first." The man hands my form and ID back to me, looks away from my eyes, and waves his hand at the person standing behind me to approach the counter. After what seemed to be a very personal conversation, he is finished with me.

"Wait, so that's all we can do today? I need to get my social security card first? I thought I'd come here and then bring my new license to them."

"See them first. It's easier that way."

For who? I think.

I walk out of the DMV completely deflated, like I have just failed my driving test. Maybe this whole thing is stupid. Maybe I should just keep my married name and not put myself through all of this.

But then I remember.

I turn up the music and remember why I need to take myself back. I remember shifting my identity so far into what my husband wanted me to be that I completely forgot who I was. I remember doing the same for my parents growing up, attempting to become the perfect daughter, the perfect sister, and never allowing myself to just BE. Then, when I met my dominant husband, it felt natural and only right that I continue my morphing into the perfect wife and mother. I had no idea who I was anymore; maybe I never allowed myself to find out.

But I know my name. And for some reason taking my name back seems to threaten other people's choices and beliefs. But that doesn't mean it's the wrong action for me to take. I don't have to give up.

After a series of strenuous yoga flows and postures, I always look forward to when the instructor says, "Now we will come down to the mat."

Coming down into dandasana (staff pose) signals an acknowledgment of effort that has been made. After moving through several standing postures, class is not over, and there is plenty of work to be done in seated postures, but in the lowering, the coming down, I taste a bit of relief that much of the effort is complete. A new imprint has been made, a budding has begun.

The closest Social Security Agency is forty-five minutes away, and after following the directions on my phone, I end up in what appears to be a rough part of the city. Abandoned buildings line the sidewalk and clumps of young people suspiciously decorate each corner. I see no shops with window displays and no restaurants for a lunch crowd, despite it being 12:30 on a Thursday.

I find the SSA, which has the only full parking lot within miles, and I walk in. I wind myself through a revolving door and into a small glass cell where a police officer stands at a beige-colored podium.

"I need to ask why you are here."

"Oh, I'm changing my name." I reply, as I begin removing the heavy folder from my bag that contains all my evidence.

"Marriage?" He asks.

"No, divorce."

He doesn't respond or ask me for my folder or anything else. He hands me a thin white ticket with a number on it and opens an adjacent glass door that leads to a small, comfortable-looking waiting room. The people seated here are much more lively than everyone at the DMV. Parents sit with small children and occupy them with books and games. An Indian woman in a colorful sari smiles at me when I walk in. She gestures to me that the seat next to hers is open. I sit down and say thank you. I notice her Nike sneakers under the ornate, silky fabric of her sari.

I set my ticket on the armrest of my chair so I won't forget my number, and I thumb through the documents in my folder, double checking I have everything I could possibly need. Birth certificate, marriage license, divorce decree. I wonder silently if I should have brought Nicole's love letters to David as proof of why I am here.

When my number is called, I stand up and see a woman waving me toward her. She directs me into a small room and shuts the door behind me as I sit down in a comfortable chair in front of a large desk. I have no idea what is about to happen. I feel like I have just walked into a job interview. I place my folder on the desk, sit up straight, adjust my shoulders back, and inhale deeply.

"Welcome!" the woman says. I like her smile and her big earrings. They match her bright red pants, and I notice the sparkly jewels on her shoes before she sits back down behind her impressive desk.

"Nice shoes," I comment.

"Well, thank you! My daughters gave them to me. Lord, do we love our shoes!" she laughs.

I like her. The name on her desk plaque says Charlotte.

Charlotte asks me if I brought my divorce decree, and I hand her the thirty-page file. Using the eraser on the back of her pencil, she flips quickly to page twenty-one where there is a line that says: "subject (wife) to reinstate her maiden name." She spins her pencil around and checks the spot lightly, then types quietly at her computer.

"Do you have a birth certificate?"

"Yes." I hand it to her.

Charlotte types some more.

I wait, with no faith that I have brought the correct documents. I wonder what I will need to defend today. Why did I get divorced again? Was it the affair? Or was it the marriage overall? Was I unhappy the entire time? When did it start to become unhealthy? Was it ever love, or was I grieving something that never actually existed in the first place?

I stretch my spine and my crown upward in dandasana, the easiest/ hardest pose ever. It simply looks like a person sitting on the floor, like the L-shaped staff in music—my back straight, legs extended in front of me. No one would take a photo of staff pose or put it on the cover of a yoga magazine. Regardless of how the pose appears, I push my muscles to do the work needed in order keep my legs and back straight, both stretching and reaching equally in opposite directions to hold on to the pose. I press the backs of my knees closer to the ground, and I continually pull up on my top thigh muscles, making sure my hips rotate slightly inward. I pull in on my lower abdominals and engage my low back, in order to support my erect spine. In reality, sitting in staff pose takes an extreme amount of work, unless you fake it, which is also an option, and one that no one would catch on to.

My thigh muscles quiver and shake. I flex my feet further back to point all my toes upward. The backs of my calves begin to burn. I crave the folding over, when the effort will end and the release will begin.

As Charlotte continues typing, the flesh on the back of my neck burns, like I am in trouble. I think of the drive here and the drive back home. I think of the waiting room and the smiling woman sitting next to me; I wonder what her story is.

Logically, I know I haven't done anything wrong, but that same feeling is there a the back of my neck. Doubt settles in, my familiar emotion. How did I get here?

Charlotte presses one more key on her computer. Then, satisfied, her eyes look up and meet mine. She folds her hands together on top of her shiny desk and smiles. "OK, you're all set! Just look for an envelope in the mail in a few weeks."

"Wow, that's it?" I say, surprised, vindicated, and relieved, like I have just been given permission to fold over my legs in staff pose, to retreat to a place of calm and complete an exhale after all the hard work and trying. Charlotte stands up and walks to the door. She opens it and extends her other hand to shake mine before I leave.

I fold all the way forward in staff pose and allow my spine to curve and my back to release. My legs naturally let go and my forehead lowers closer to my knees. I roll slowly backward and use my core muscles to come down onto my back. I lay down on my mat and bend my knees until my body is in a little ball. I inhale fully into my belly and extend both legs and arms outward, into starfish pose. My entire abdomen tightens and ripples as it holds my limbs outward and just slightly off the floor. I crouch back into a ball as I exhale and release everything out again, several times. I inhale and exhale, open and close until my core burns and shakes and reminds me of all the muscles under my skin and around my organs. I lay back for the last time and let my legs and arms fall to meet the floor. I relax every single muscle and cell in my body. I allow my feet to open out to the sides. I let go in my inner thighs and my lower back. I drop the heavy bones of my hips and shoulders down onto the mat. I loosen my face and jaw. My ab muscles continue to flex slightly, even with my arms and legs now resting and limp. My body and core continue to support me even while lying down. Even while letting go, the sensation of strength in my body remains. For now, I am ready for rest. Satisfied, I close my eyes and exhale.

Acknowledgments

In June 2017, I blindly followed my heart and attended Write by the Lake, a weeklong writing course in Madison, Wisconsin. Despite not even having a book idea, I took a class with Julie Tallard Johnson called Write Meaningful Nonfiction: Turn Your Personal Experience into a Book. "What's your book about?" Julie asked when I was the first to arrive. "I'm not sure," I answered, intimidated by the question. "You'll know. By the end of the week, you'll know." She glided away to greet another student.

This one decision changed the course of my life, as often happens when we take one tiny step in response to our intuition. The next few years would be dark and challenging. Writing, and Julie's circles, truly saved my life. Thank you, Julie, for believing in me from day one and for creating sacred spaces for writers to emerge and heal.

I am forever grateful for my very first writing partner, Katy Phillips, a beautiful soul and poet. Thank you to my magical writing circle of fierce and powerful women, for your instrumental support in writing and in life: Mary, Lizzy (Betty), Kim, Cammy, Susan, Patty, Jess, Francie, and Dona. Thank you to my childhood friends for loving me when I couldn't love myself: Sarah, Kelly, Chandelle, Kate, and Megan. Thank you to Kimberly Lempart; you are the dearest, most unexpected friend, and I treasure the destiny of when our paths crossed. Thank you to Katie Butcher for being my biggest cheerleader while writing.

I am grateful for my beautiful recovery community who have shared themselves so freely and given me the courage to heal.

I am grateful for my parents, Bob and Jean Chanson, my sister Anne, my brother Jake, and my sister-in-law Jackie who have been there for me through the great times and the terrible and have supported me with unconditional love. I can't imagine going through life without us.

A very special thank you to Nick Ades for encouraging my writing and for giving me the opportunity to discover my own strength. You are the best co-parent on this unconventional path. Thank you to our boys, Bennett and Andrew, who are my inspiration to be a better person.

Thank you to everyone at Kripalu Center for Yoga and Health for sharing the wisdom of compassionate yoga so that others may go out and heal the world. A special thank you to my YTT teachers, Yoganand Michael Carroll and Janna Delgado, for reading my manuscript and offering feedback. Thank you to Stephen Cope for responding to my crazy email and taking a chance on a new author. Your book, *Yoga and the Quest for the True Self* inspired me in 2001. You are a pioneer in sharing the teachings of yoga for life, and I am honored to now call you a friend.

Finally, thank you to my Steve, for being you.

Sources

[21] Sri Swami Satchidananda. *The Yoga Sutras of Patanjali.* Integral Yoga Publications, 2012.

[23] Drake, R. M. www.rmdrake.com [@rmdrk Instagram profile] 2017.

[29] Deborah Adele. *The Yamas and Niyamas: Exploring Yoga's Ethical Practice.* On-Word Bound Books, 2009.

[37] Libba Bray. *Beauty Queens.* Scholastic Incorporated, 2011.

[43] Satchidananda.

[49] Sylvia Plath. *The Bell Jar: A Novel.* HarperCollins, 2015.

[65] Jon and Myla Kabat-Zinn. *Everyday Blessings: The Inner Work of Mindful Parenting.* Hatchette Books, 1997.

[73] Rebecca Campbell. *Rise Sister Rise: A Guide to Unleashing the Wise, Wild Woman Within.* Hay House, 2016.

[83] Swami Kripalvanandji and Atma Jo Ann Levitt. *Pilgrims of Love: The Life and Teachings of Swami Kripalu.* Monkfish Book Publishing. 2004.

[89] Satchidananda.

[95] Rolf Gates and Katrina Kenison. *Meditations from the Mat: Daily Reflections on the Path of Yoga.* Anchor Books, 2002.

[97] Eckhart Tolle. *A New Earth.* Penguin, 2005.

[109] Markus Zusak. *The Book Thief.* Alfred A. Knopf, 2005.

[111] George P. Shultz and William E. Simon. *A Time for Reflection: An Autobiography.* Regnery Publishing, 2013.

[117] Stephen Cope. *Yoga and the Quest for the True Self.* Bantam Books, 1999.

[119] Elizabeth Gilbert. *Eat, Pray, Love.* Penguin, 2006.

[125] Nelle Morton. *The Journey is Home.*

[131] Satchidananda.

[143] Satchidananda.

[145] Rameshwar Das. *Polishing the Mirror: How to Live from Your Spiritual Heart.* Sounds True, 2013.

[153] James Robertshaw. *First Native Americans: Culture & History.* James Robertshaw, 2021.

[161] Nausicaa Twila. *Beautiful Minds Anonymous.* Lulu.com Self Publishing, 2015.

[169] Satchidananda.

[171] Satchidananda.

[177] Virginia Woolf. *A Room of One's Own.* Hogarth Press, 1929.

[185] C. S. Lewis. *Mere Christianity.* HarperOne, 1996.

[193] Joseph P. Kauffman. *The Answer Is YOU: A Guide to Mental, Emotional, and Spiritual Freedom.* Conscious Collective, LLC, 2017.

[195] Nausicaa Twila. *Beautiful Minds Anonymous.* Lulu.com, 2015.

[205] Deepak Chopra. *The Seven Spiritual Laws of Success: A Practical Guide to the Fulfillment of Your Dreams.* Createspace Independent Pub, 2009.

OTHER REFERENCES

Pema Chödrön. *When Things Fall Apart: Heart Advice for Difficult Times.* Shambhala, 2016.

Patrick J. Carnes. *The Betrayal Bond: Breaking Free of Exploitive Relationships.* Health Communications Inc, 1997.

Debbie Ford. *The Dark Side of the Light Chasers: Reclaiming your Power, Creativity, Brilliance, and Dreams.* Riverhead Books, 1998.

Julie Tallard Johnson. *The Zero Point Agreement: How To Be Who You Already Are.* Destiny Books, 2013.

Dharma Singh Khalsa and Cameron Stauth. *Meditation as Medicine: Activate the Power of Your Natural Healing Force.* Atria, 2002.

Allison Gemmel Laframboise with Yoganand Michael Carrol. *Pranayama: A Path to Healing and Freedom.* CreateSpace, 2015.

Tosha Silver. *Outrageous Openness: Letting the Divine Take the Lead.* Atria, 2014.

Charlotte A. Tomaino. *Awakening the Brain: The Neuropsychology of Grace*. Atria, 2012.

Bessel Van Der Kolk. *The Body Keeps the Score: Brain, Mind, and Body in the Healing of Trauma*. Penguin, 2015.

Marianne Williamson. *A Return to Love: Reflections on the Principles of a Course in Miracles*. Harper Colins, 1992.

About the Author

Molly Chanson is a writer, teacher, and yoga instructor who shares the physical and ethical practices of yoga as a way to heal, overcome difficulty, and live a fulfilled life. Molly holds a bachelor's degree from the University of Wisconsin–Madison and a master's degree from the University of Illinois at Chicago. Molly taught in the English department at Columbia College Chicago for fourteen years before moving back to her hometown in Wisconsin to raise her two boys. In 2019 Molly completed her 200-hour Yoga Teacher Training at Kripalu Center for Yoga and Health, a leader in yoga and mindfulness-based education for over fifty years. Molly is founder of The Practice, an online yoga membership that offers yoga, writing, and spiritual teachings based on the philosophies of yoga as a path to transformation. This is Molly's first book. To learn more or take a class, visit www.mollychanson.com.

SHANTI ARTS

NATURE ▪ ART ▪ SPIRIT

Please visit us online
to browse our entire book catalog,
including poetry collections and fiction,
books on travel, nature, healing, art,
photography, and more.

Also take a look at our highly regarded art
and literary journal, *Still Point Arts Quarterly*,
which may be downloaded for free.

www.shantiarts.com

CPSIA information can be obtained
at www.ICGtesting.com
Printed in the USA
BVHW031209260422
635370BV00003B/47